Family Camping

Family Camping

Handbook for Parents

by

LLOYD D. MATTSON

MOODY PRESS

CHICAGO

Contents

Introduction

FAMILY CAMPING—there is a nice ring to that. It calls forth
pictures of Mom, Dad, and the kids seated around a campfire roasting marshmallows. Or maybe you picture a bright
orange tent nestled in a valley with trout sizzling in the
frying pan. It may bring ideas of a travel trailer parked by
the ocean with the family splashing in the surf, a thousand
miles from the office.

America and Europe are caught up in a family camping
boom unlike anything ever witnessed before. The recreation vehicle industry cannot keep up with the demand, and
many a farmer has converted his fields into campsites, turn-
ing a tidy dollar in the process.

How do you account for this return to nature? This generation has witnessed a man walking on the moon, supported by a technology so advanced the layman cannot
imagine it. Camping is hardly a worship of technology!
Electronic entertainment zooms upward, spectator sports
set new attendance and dollar records, yet each season
more millions are taking to the highways and trails.

Why? Perhaps affluence and gadgets have made possible more time for recreation. Perhaps a hidden instinct is
driving people into a world they had forgotten, the world
of nature and simple living, where people must depend on
one another and learn self-reliance at the same time. What-

ever the reasons, families are camping in unprecedented numbers. Among them are thousands of Christian families. This is one of the most encouraging signs to be found.

The values of camping for the Christian family represent the burden of this writing. Camping is fun in itself for those who enjoy the outdoors. But camping is more than fun. Camping is perhaps the best opportunity a family has to discover its own spiritual identity in a day like ours.

You will find this an intensely personal book, for camping is a personal activity. Pack frames and wedge tents can be described with clinical objectivity, but the human values inherent in camping demand the first person.

You may find preachy passages—an unforgivable literary sin, I am told. Skim over those passages if you will, but I write from the vantage point of a Christian, a churchman, a family man, and a camper. It has been my privilege to serve as a pastor, a denominational staff member and now a professional camper. I love the church and the outdoors. I see no conflict between disciplined family camping and good churchmanship.

Along with the *why* of Christian family camping, we will discuss the *where* and *how* of family camping in several settings. If you are a veteran camper, you will not likely find anything new here about camping techniques. I hope, though, that you will find challenge and help in the aspects of this book that deal with the benefits of camping for the Christian family.

1

The Church in Your House

How you view churchmanship concerns me, for many have failed to discover the most important church they serve. We know about the universal church, that mystic body of all God's children everywhere. And we are familiar with the church on the corner where we worship and serve together. But some have failed to recognize the small congregation that meets day after day under one roof, your house. That is the church that stands to gain from family camping. And when the church at your house prospers, the church on the corner will prosper too.

LOOKING BACK

I covet for every family the delights found by my family while out camping, and I covet for your children the riches I gained as a child through those adventures when we packed up the Model T and drove off into the wilderness.

How long ago was it? I could not have been five years old on that day Dad was securing a blanket tent-fashion over our heads, attempting to thwart the northern Wisconsin mosquitos. I cannot recall the mosquitos, but I fondly remember that first family camp-out.

I recall the curious brown cows staring across the fence at my nervous sister. I remember the log dam and dark

river water where I first learned about fishing, the lemon-
ade and homemade biscuits, and the scolding I got for
eating the heap off the pail of blueberries.

Dad built more than a blanket on the porch that summer
evening. He was building his church, the church that met
at his house. It was a good church too. Whatever we
lacked in formal religious exercises was more than com-
pensated for by scores of small adventures.

From my parents' home sprang four Christian families
with grandchildren and great-grandchildren who follow
God's ways.

I do not suggest that camping alone builds the family
nor that noncamping families must fail. I am suggesting
that the quality of life experienced while camping permits
children and parents to enter new relationships where primary Christianity can be observed.

It is dreadfully easy to practice secondhand Christianity.
The pressures of work, school, and community life are in-
tensified by a demanding church schedule. There seems
to be no cure for the inordinate busyness afflicting people
today. Certainly the church faces a crushing assignment,
maintaining past traditions and struggling to keep abreast
of new developments. And the most harried of all are the
ministers. Maybe it is time for someone to take a fresh
look at the Christian in the real world of today. Worship
can easily become mere ritual, a secondhand encounter.

THE OTHER CHURCH

Twenty-five years ago I pastored a small church in
northern Michigan. The winters were long and snow-
filled. I looked forward to spring because trout season

opened and because vacationing families would return soon.

My largest congregations gathered in July and August. We forced back the ancient folding doors to open the overflow room. Our Sunday school boomed, and even the church treasurer wore a smile. Families camping in our vacation country were a boon to my small church, but I understand there were grumblings in the churches back in Chicago!

Some years later I served a church in a larger city, and now I understand. However beloved the visiting family might be out in the hinterlands, vacations do nothing for the statistics back home.

But two kinds of statistics must be reconciled. One appears on the attendance and offering record back home in the church building. The other is more subtle, appearing in the hearts of family members. This is the other church for which every Christian parent bears primary responsibility. Of this you can be positive: God never requires you to fail Him in one duty while honoring Him in another. A healthy Christian family will never frustrate God's plan for a healthy home church.

I understand now that the church extends beyond the perimeter of masonry and calendar that meant so much to me as a young minister. As my pastoral years moved along, I became less concerned about people as Sunday statistics and adjuncts to my programs, and more concerned that they find God's fullest joy as individuals and families. Occasionally this required that they be absent on Sunday, maybe to go camping.

Certainly the Christian family will own a church home.

But the church does not own families! The church exists for the home and that other church that lives there. The pastor whose benediction follows the family when they go camping ministers in a mighty way even though Mom, Dad, and the children miss the Sunday sermon.

PASTOR DAD

Let me lay the burden on you, Dad. You have an assignment from heaven and your days are numbered. God has provided all you need to fulfill your assignment, and you cannot hire anyone to take your place. You must minister to the church in your home.

A few years ago I preached at a men's retreat in Iowa. My talks, as often happens, were sprinkled with anecdotes from my boyhood. I challenged the men to make life worth living for their kids. Following one session a middle-aged man approached me. "Know why I can't talk about my boyhood?" he said. "I never had one." He walked away sadly.

I know a lot of men like that. Their dads were often good providers and proper church members. They never beat their wives or children. They may have been deacons or ministers, yet their sons had no boyhood worth remembering.

Come to think of it, a dad like that has very little to remember himself! The wealth of mature years are memories. I can remember occasions when I disappointed my children because someone called a last-minute committee meeting. I cannot remember what the committee discussed, but I remember my disappointed children. I excused myself on the grounds that the committee represented God's work, and I squandered a memory.

As I write, on my shelves I see the memorabilia of my near half century. There is a beaver jaw up there with its arching white chisel. I picked it up along the Grays River not far from the Box Y where our family spent unforgettable weeks with Sam and Ila Young. Next to the beaver jaw is a six-inch chunk of spruce, chewed off by a Canadian beaver, retrieved from an Ontario stream one autumn. Then there is a smoke-darkened figure carved by Darrell Bellville's son in the high cascades. A chunk of fossil, petrified wood, a pair of beaded, sealskin moccasins made by some Eskimo lady and sent to me by friends from Alaska when I needed a lift.

These are good things, and I cherish them. Yet, if they were lost, my sorrow would be brief; for associated with each souvenir are memories that will last as long as I do, and I like to think I might even chuckle over some of them in heaven!

I see clearly in my memory my wife and sons riding into a sheepherder's camp in Blind Bull Canyon, not far from where I found the beaver's jaw. I hear my son's song and the strumming of his guitar around a score of campfires. I think often of that camp-out along Deep Creek in Alaska which I will tell you about by and by.

Camping has afforded us fantastic adventures, like bouncing down a river in rubber rafts. It has also been the means by which we have formed so many close friendships. I am certain that our children are not the only ones who have profited from our camping trips. All but one of our children are gone now, and we have five grandchildren.

Our memory-gathering days with our family are pretty well spent, but we have so many wonderful times to remember.

If a father is to fulfill his role as the pastor of the family, then he must create the kind of relationships where the family can learn true worship.

Children must do more than hear sound theology and learn the right memory verses. They must see that Christ does make a difference, that the Christian life is *real* life. To do this, they must do some firsthand living with the most influential Christians in the world, their parents.

If we are serious about Christian family life, then some means must be found to help our children discover the reality of the gospel in firsthand living. In my opinion there is hardly any kind of living so firsthand as family camping.

A group of junior boys taught me anew the best way to kindle a fire. We were camping in the magnificent firs in the Pacific Northwest, and I had given instruction in campfire cookery. The lads had been little impressed by my illustrated lecture on fire building and preparations for cooking a foil dinner, and they howled with dismay when I informed them they had only two matches to build their fire. If they failed, they would eat raw food.

Meanwhile, my fire blazed away as I fed coals to the swelling envelope of foil which contained my dinner. The boys were scattered about in pairs building their fires. Groans from here and there indicated that not all was going well.

Finally one boy approached me, his face marked with sorrow. "Cap, could I talk to you a minute?" he asked.

I steeled my resolve to yield no more matches. He led me to the edge of the clearing and took a position that made it necessary for me to turn my back to my fire. The lad poured out a disconnected tale of woes which I pounced on with all manner of good advice. "Thanks, Cap," he said finally. "You've helped me a lot."

I had no idea how much I had helped him, for when I returned to my fire, it was all but gone. In the small clearing five other fires blazed. The boys discovered that borrowed matches may not do the job, but when you start with live coals and breathe gently on the tinder, you get fire!

A similar kindling reaction occurs when the family camps together. Children see their parents in a new light. The pastoral role of the father finds many occasions for fulfillment as the family breaks out of its busy routine. The fire of God's love and purposes can be passed from parent to child, fanned by the father's prayers.

CAMPING: A CHANGE OF PACE

Camping certainly breaks family routine! A skunk sniffing your food box at early dawn is quite a change, and as the family dog notices him, you may be reminded of the importance of prayer. A sudden downpour with the tent half-pitched brings togetherness like nothing else your family can experience.

Family camping shrinks the generation gap, too, a gap some adults fail to realize is caused by movement in two directions. Dad and Mom take on new personalities in camp. They are less fussy, hopefully, and probably less confident. Both young people and parents find the generation gap is primarily a communication short circuit. Differences in viewpoint can make wholesome discussion topics if people are talking and listening to one another.

Some children have never heard their fathers talk about their spiritual struggles. These children assume that their fathers always possessed a rock-solid faith and have no problems now. Dad knows better. Talking comes naturally when you allow time for it. How much conversation time do you find around home?

Camping leisurely gives families an opportunity to play, sing, and talk together. Perhaps it is because the barriers of the familiar are breached, freeing parents and children to talk as friends. It also gives families a chance to make prayer and worship simple and natural, rather than struggling for the right mood or atmosphere imposed on an otherwise unworshipful life tone.

Children might discover that being a Christian is not something that happens at stated hours in certain buildings, but that Jesus is exactly the same when you play as when you pray. No hour is more spiritual than another, though some hours are sober and others lighthearted. They might learn that worship is a welling up of love for the God of heaven, who made mountains and streams, and who gave them their parents.

It would be worthwhile for parents to rediscover these ideas too. Family camping and other family activity of primary interest to the children will help establish a personal spiritual identity which will not be lost when the children leave for college. As children feel the warmth of God's love in their parents, they will kindle their own fires of faith.

CAMPING IS DOING

There is another dimension to camping that serves our generation well. We have become a world of spectators. If you want to measure the depth of our need for something to watch, note the salaries paid professional athletes and other entertainers. Camping thrusts the individual back into the elementary world of doing.

Camping offers a personal challenge to our flabby generation. Families can work together making a camp, climbing a hill, portaging a canoe, or preparing meals. Every camper becomes a participant; there are no mere spectators.

Much has been written in recent years concerning the value of stress experiences in camping. Rigorous programs test campers to their physical and mental limits. I don't advocate this for a short-term family camp, but we see a parallel in values. Should we degenerate to the point where a ten-mile hike becomes impossible, even for Dad and Mom?

My favorite scene from many father-son camping trips occurred one morning in the Wyoming range. The lad was perhaps ten years old and obviously not accustomed to strenuous work. He was in that limbo between childhood and growing up: too old to cry and too young to be tough. The day grew uncomfortably hot and the nine-thousand-foot altitude took its toll.

Our route carried us across a series of high ridges with uncommonly steep approaches. All of us felt the weariness growing, but there was no way out but hiking. I paused to catch my breath and watched the lad staggering slowly under his pack. The weight was modest, and his condition quite obviously exaggerated. I suspected that some of his acting was meant to be seen by his father, who was following.

Without a word the lad communicated his desperate condition. His melting brown eyes pleaded, *Dad, please take my pack.*

But his father surprised both me and the boy. He swung past the lad, saying, "Let's go, son. Just another mile and a half." He left the boy dumbfounded and with no choice except to plod on. That boy grew up in the next two hours. He made it under his own power and carried his own pack too.

A New World for Dad

Let me add a final value to be found in family camping. Both the family and Dad benefit when he discovers that he does not have to be the best in every way. It takes a big man to risk failure when he can avoid it, and camping inevitably brings risk.

A boy spoke up one evening as we were discussing parent-son relationships. "If just once my dad would admit he was wrong, maybe we could get along," he said. The bitterness was evident. Pity the father who must always be right!

Camping offers parents an opportunity to become vulnerable, to join the children in an uncertain world. Where else in family life is this possible? If a youngster can solve a problem that baffles Dad, points are made for Dad!

Camping must be classified as an art rather than a science. The skills are never fully mastered, for the variables are too many. As the family learns camping together, children discover the person behind the father image. The busy, efficient, off-to-work attitude men so easily assume around home melts away over a campfire, especially when Junior informs him that big fires are for sitting around, little fires are for cooking.

The Christian parents' ultimate purpose blends with the goals of the church, to present ourselves and our children complete in Christ. We covet for our children a personal, vital faith that transcends the pressures of new environments and peer groups. We seek an open friendship where love can heal small and big wounds. We look for that place where the spirit of the law overtakes the letter, where Christianity becomes life rather than mere religion.

Can family camping accomplish all this? Of course not, not in some magical way. But camping does offer a setting where these discoveries can take place, for camping takes the family out of the familiar surroundings of the home and neighborhood into a new world where parents and children can share basic living. If there the parents live as genuine Christians before their children, the church in their house will thrive.

2

Camping Is Everywhere

THE BOYS AND I were fishing in Dagger Lake in the North Cascades one August evening when a distant whinny told us riders were approaching. We watched a dozen horses work their way down a steep slope. The last rider led a pack string. These were no dudes! They eased from their saddles and began setting up camp with evident skill.

After the pack animals were unloaded, they rolled with delight. The riders strung the saddles along a fallen log. Before long, the fire was blazing and a smokey coffeepot marked the official establishment of the night's camp. We gave them a string of trout and hiked off toward our camp.

There two families enjoying their mountain country, camping as their forefathers had before them, made a delightful scene.

A day or so later we came across another family. They were backpackers: mother, father, and two teenage girls. Their trip would extend for three weeks! Food caches awaited them at prearranged points, lightening their packs. But their hike would take them nearly two hundred miles through the mountains. Their clothes were dusty and worn, but their refreshing smiles and their ease with one another suggested that camping was good for their family.

Family camping offers a sufficient variety of experiences

to satisfy almost every level of interest. You may not feel qualified to hike through the mountains or take off on a canoe trip without a guide. But this is no barrier to meaningful family adventure. The degree of creature comfort you enjoy depends solely on your tastes and pocketbook.

The first camping trip I recall, which I mentioned in the first chapter, carried us all of forty miles, a long ride in a Model T. We camped because motels had not yet been invented, nor had the age of affluence come upon us. My parents sought for blueberries in the Wisconsin swamps, and camping out was the only way respectable blueberry pickers knew how to spend the night.

Thirty some years later I took my family on our longest camping trip to date. We covered about fifteen thousand miles over nine weeks: from Alaska through the Midwest, to California and back through British Columbia to Alaska. The value of family camping lies in its versatility. You can go as far as you wish. A stay within ten miles of home will provide essentially the basic experiences, and new skill will be gained with each trip.

KINDS OF FAMILY CAMPING

In this book we are concerned primarily with the Christian family camping on its own. However, we will discuss group family camping in chapter 9, and briefly mention several kinds of camping you can enjoy in this chapter.

The first Christian camp on record in the New World, as far as I can determine, was the Cane Ridge Camp Meeting, Cane Ridge, Kentucky, established around 1801. That was a family camp. Most Christian camps for the next century seem to have offered adult-oriented family programs.

Then youth camps developed, and they dominated interest for thirty years.

Today family camping is the fastest growing dimension of the Christian camp movement. Bible camps find family weeks filled months in advance, and more weeks for families are being added. A few years ago the future looked bleak for some of America's historic Bible conferences. Today many are booming as they turn to programming for families.

Many camps have developed modern sites to serve the growing number of families who own recreation vehicles. They are invited to visit for a day or two, or to bring their camper of trailer to supplement the limited cabin facilities during family weeks.

Carefully programmed family camps offer a rewarding experience for families who have enjoyed a variety of independent camping trips. More about this in chapter 9.

Many churches become involved in caravan camping each year. Families provide their own vehicles and camping equipment, meeting at a public or private campground for several days or a week. The program usually includes informal gatherings once or twice a day, with each family caring for its own camping and recreational needs. The long weekend is a favorite time for caravan camping.

The word *caravan* should not imply that the group travels together, a practice not recommended because of safety factors. Rarely does the group attempt to move from place to place. But rather, a rendezvous point is designated and families arrive or depart at their convenience. The church caravan camp provides valuable opportunities for fellowship in another setting in our fast-moving society.

Family camping rallies attract thousands of people each year. Christian family camping fellowships have sprung up, and others are certain to follow. The largest at this writing is probably Campers on Mission, sponsored by the Southern Baptists but open to all Christian families. National and regional rallies bring together an impressive number of Christians for fellowship and witness.

The tendency for families to join other families for camping adventure indicates that a hunger for isolation is not the only motivation behind the surge in family camping interest. But for many, camping reaches its zenith when the family locks the house door and heads for the open spaces on its own.

JUST MOM, DAD AND THE KIDS

If you have looked for waterfront property lately, you know that interest in the vacation cottage has not declined. A week at the lake, which is still popluar among many families, has many of the values of camping. Private cottages may be rented; or the family may build a cottage, adding the value of working together.

Some families find, however, that a lakeside cottage invites a stream of friends who drop by, often unannounced. Mom may work harder entertaining guests than she works at home! The labor and expense of maintaining a summer cottage has discouraged many families. They have turned to other kinds of holiday sites, such as vacation lodges.

Scattered throughout the country are many types of family vacation centers. Not far from Chicago, you can spend a week at a working farm, circa 1910. The vacation farm idea probably grew out of the many successful dude ranches where families can enjoy riding, watching cowboys at work, and other traditional Western activities.

Wherever you find lakes and ocean frontage, you will find fishing and water sports centers offering vacation accommodations. Some of these include side trips of several days' duration. In some parts of the country you can find vacation lodges operated by Christians with activities of special interest for families.

Some will wonder if a week at a lodge qualifies as family camping. Whenever the family shares in recreation and adventure away from home, the values of family camping are found. Tastes in vacations vary widely, with some preferring the complete relaxation found in a lodge. Others enjoy a housekeeping cabin, or the do-it-yourself approach of tent or trailer camping. Still others like rugged wilderness trips. The kind of experience is less important than the fact that a family spends time together away from the routine of home, sharing whatever the circumstances demand.

THE OPEN ROAD

A combination of factors gave rise to the amazing growth in family camping which began slowly and reached a frenzy in the late 1960s. Visit a vacation show in any city and you will be staggered by the immensity of the recreation vehicle industry. From trim, low camper trailers to huge mobile homes, millions of families are taking to the open road.

The early years found campers hunting a place to park in public campgrounds as night approached. But soon businessmen discovered camping. Today you will find

franchise and independent camping parks springing up everywhere. Farmers have converted cornfields; motel chains
are opening parks. Yet there is little hope in the early 70s
that park development can keep pace with the manufacturers of recreation vehicles. National parks are phasing
out sites because camper pressure already has overtaxed
the areas. When you travel with your camper, it is better
to stop by midafternoon if you drive the main routes, or
you will not find a place to camp. Gradually, more park
systems will develop motellike reservation plans.

At this writing, trailer park fees are modest—from three
to five dollars per night. Water, power, and sewer hookups are available, usually at extra cost. Many parks offer
swimming pools, a store for food and supplies, recreation
centers for children and young people, fishing ponds, laun-
dry facilities and lounges.

A spirit of comradeship prevails among campers, with
clusters of neighbors sharing evening campfires. The witnessing Chistian finds ready access to the heart and ear of
fellow campers.

An interesting splinter industry is the condominium
trailer park. A family buys or leases space, then parks the
trailer permanently, driving out whenever they wish. This
is a new angle to the old summer cottage idea—an escape
from hot, crowded cities.

The recreation vehicle and superhighways put the whole
nation within practical reach of most families with two or
more vacation weeks. We will consider the advantages of
the several types of recreation rigs in the chapter that follows.

TRAVEL CAMPING VALUES

One apparent value of the recreation vehicle must be examined: that is economy. Owning and operating a recreation vehicle costs more than you might think, especially if you buy one of the better quality outfits. The family should weigh the time they plan to spend camping, for there is more to family camping than creature comforts. A rented unit or less expensive rig might be more appropriate for your needs.

A few years ago I visited a caravan camp, and among the forty families that drove in, almost every type of camping gear was represented. My attention was drawn to one family. They arrived in an attractive mobile home, complete with TV antenna and a full-length awning. The family organized lawn chairs and tables under the awning and settled down for a relaxed, comfortable stay.

Across the way another family pulled in. They brought five or six children, one of them an infant. Their shelter was a homemade box of corrugated steel and plywood huddled on the back of an ancient pickup. They pitched a small, worn tent which accommodated the overflow for sleeping. The family kindled a fire to cook their meals.

I would judge that the spread in price between the two families' outfits exceeded fifteen thousand, but their delight in sharing the camp seemed equal! The price tag on equipment has little to do with the rewards of camping. Both families drove homeward richer for having spent time with other families and with each other.

Camping along the highways opens the way for a wide variety of family discoveries. Leisurely trips are best, pausing at points of interest. Too often we make getting someplace the goal for the day. The distance we must cover demands passing by much that the family would enjoy.

On one of our trips, we drove through the Dakotas and Montana. We came to an area famed for its prairie dog villages. I pulled off the road so the children could see the quaint critters. Of course everyone wanted to get out of the car for a closer look. But I worried about reaching our destination, so we hurried on. Unfortunately, our destination offered nothing to equal an appeal of prairie dog village. I wish now we had stopped for a few minutes.

Travel camping always holds the possibility of meeting the unexpected. Driving home from Alaska, we had an experience that my wife, Elsie, and I have laughed about many times.

The sun was nowhere near cresting the hills when Elsie's urgent whisper awakened me. "Get up," she ordered. "I think there's a bear down the road." It takes a mighty exciting bear to stir my adrenalin before sunrise, even in the Yukon, but then I heard a garbage can cover clatter to the ground. I woke up. Elsie was tiptoeing, camera in hand, toward the sound as I slipped into my pants and moccasins. I caught up and we moved down the winding wooded road, expecting to observe a scavenger black bear at work.

Instead, we saw a tired-looking, swaybacked black horse. He sniffed the scattered debris at his feet. Then, lifting his head, he spotted us and ambled our way, looking pleased to find someone up so early. The horse paused in front of us, obviously expecting some toll for our trespassing.

We invited him to come along to our camp, which he did. I fed him bolten biscuits while Elsie snapped a picture in the dim light. The picture did not come out so well, but we laugh each time we see it. We remember a friendly stray black horse shuffling from camp to camp as though he were the official garbage inspector. That was a good day.

Just as you pace a trail trip according to the strength of your weakest camper, plan your travel trip for the pleasure of your youngest family member. Camping must be fun, else why go? Beware of long stops that hold interest only for adults. Provide pleasant diversion for the children too, or the value of the day will be lost.

Up in our attic rests an old sheet metal cylinder, a memento from a Yukon riverboat. My two youngest boys and I were driving hard to reach Alaska, but we never passed through Whitehorse without pausing to inspect the old flat-bottomed stern-wheelers resting along the river bank. For purely scientific purposes, I allowed the boys to inspect the interior of one relic. They returned with the section of a heating or ventiltaing system found in a pile of debris on the deck.

My first impulse was to say, "Put it back. It's just junk." As far as anyone else was concerned, that was all it was— worthless, rusting junk. But to my sons it represented history. They tossed it into the van, and we hauled it all the way to Alaska and home. Now it waits in my attic. Maybe five years from now one of those boys will retrieve the treasure and mount a hi-fi speaker in it. Or maybe it just will be moved to his attic.

A recreation vehicle, no matter how simple, opens the

door for worthy family adventure. Neither the quality of the slides or the value of souvenirs reflect the worth of family camping. But when one of the grown-up children visits home and says, "Dad, remember when—" the value of our family trips finds affirmation.

Camping Under Canvas

Camping in tents seems to be as old as mankind. Tents provided cover for the migrating Israelites, and today's family campers should not spurn a shelter of such noble antecedents. The tent, of course, is a part of the travel camping pattern, with the chief values being romance and economy.

While I have degenerated to the travel trailer class, I still enjoy tent camping. We own several for various purposes, but our nine-by-seven-foot canoe country wedge tent finds a warm spot in my heart.

Tent camping demands a bit more organization and time, and rain can dampen even the staunchest spirits. But I challenge anyone to beat my crew at setting up camp, regardless of the rig they drive. On a trip with my sons, Dave and Kevin, we decided to see how long it took to set up camp and get to bed. We had eaten supper earlier, so there was no need to set up the camp kitchen. From the moment our van stopped rolling until we were in our sleeping bags, only twelve minutes elapsed. Pitching a tent goes quickly when you practice.

You can buy a good family tent for under one hundred dollars, and with some care it will last many seasons. We will discuss tents more in detail in the next chapter. Now we will look at another kind of family adventure.

OFF THE BEATEN TRACK

So far we have thought of family camping mainly in terms of a cabin by the lake, or a cabin on wheels—the recreation vehicle or tent transported by auto—at a trailer park or along highways. You have another camping option, usually found in combination with one of the others. Why not take your family off the beaten track?

A few summers ago Elsie and I led a dozen young people on a bike hike along Wisconsin's famed bikeway. We covered three hundred miles in six days, camping in public and private parks enroute.

Along the way we encountered a family: a father, a mother and two boys about two and four years old. The boys perched on carriers behind their parents. They planned to ride about two hundred miles, staying in motels in the small towns.

The bike boom, which began in the late 60s, continues to flourish at this writing. For the first time in decades, more bikes are being sold for adult use than for children. Bike camping can be a wonderful family adventure and the trail skills common to camping patterns discussed in chapter 7 apply here.

A variation of the bike camp is the motorbike trip. In snow country, some families have experimented with snowmobile camp-outs. The principle of the family enjoying the outdoors is the common ingredient in all varieties of trail camping.

I confess my favorite kind of family camping carries us into the wilderness by canoe or on horseback, on skis or snowshoes or on foot with a backpack. These days, it is all but impossible to find real isolation without moving far from the trails or heading down the northernmost rivers in Canada. There are spots in Alaska so remote that you must keep your wits about you or become thoroughly lost. But even there the wilderness traveler will find others seeking the same solitude.

I have met fathers carrying youngsters papoose-fashion across portages, families riding their horses through the mountains, and hiking families in great numbers. In my opinion, wilderness camping with the family provides the ultimate in outdoor adventure, and I recommend it highly.

FROM NATIONAL FOREST TO COUNTY PARK

I have been privileged to camp from Alaska to Mexico, and from Maine to British Columbia. I have enjoyed most of the wilderness areas of North America at one time or another. Yet some of my more enjoyable family camping has taken place within a half-hour drive of home.

A decade from now our wilderness will be rationed. The multitude of campers seeking adventure are wearing out the accessible trails. The famed scenic parks—Yellowstone, Grand Canyon, Yosemite, and the others—deserve your attention, but they may be out of your time allowance and budget. Do not be discouraged! You may find as much privacy and unscarred forest within your state as you could find in any of the national parks.

Among the millions of acres of public lands, you will discover state and county campgrounds which offer every camping experience you can find in the travel brochures, except the scenery. Many families have waited too long for that super trip; and by the time they got around to it, the children had passed into the years when camping with Mom and Dad held little appeal.

Start camping with your children when they are young and the habit can grow. Both parents and camp sponsors make a mistake when they wait until kids reach high school to offer the more adventurous kinds of camping.

Camping with a Purpose

When camping skills have been sharpened, you may find a blend of camping and mission most rewarding. Why not consult your mission leaders about a missionary education tour? Do not expect the missionary to host you—he is too busy to operate a tourist bureau. But why not offer some service to him?

You might assist home missionaries, for instance, those to migrant labor camps. Your family may have skills the missionary can use. Perhaps you can play or sing, or bring a fresh supply of films along. You may contact the missionary in advance about his building or repair needs. Your family could paint the missionary's home or chapel. Plan to buy supplies locally, and provide your own housing and meals. Check carefully with authorities to meet custom and entry regulations if you plan to cross a national border. Above all, do not become a burden to the mission.

Throughout rural America and Canada struggling churches and small camps would be delighted if a family were to offer help. You might establish camp nearby and conduct a vacation Bible school, or minister as camp counselors. Possibly you could serve a pastor for a week or two as his work crew. Invite his young people to your camp for a cookout. This is camping with purpose, a growing experience for families.

Perhaps you could volunteer a service project for a park manager. I saw one man and wife making a trip across a portage on Knife Lake in the canoe country. They had carried all their gear over and returned to pick up debris along the trail. They filled a pack full of litter left behind by less thoughtful campers.

SOURCES FOR INFORMATION

The list of sources of information and equipment at the back of this book gives several sources for planning family camping trips, and you will find public information sources in every region of the United States and Canada. A letter addressed to the tourist bureau of your chosen region will bring you information. The chamber of commerce will often inundate you with brochures. Many government departments publish guides for travelers and campers. Their addresses appear in the list of sources of information.

3

Choosing Your Camping Shelter

ONE OF THE SURPRISES you encounter as you drive in the far North in midsummer comes at evening. Your watch reports the onset of night, but the light remains, even though the sun has set. Full darkness never comes. We pitched our first camp in Alaska with a sense of awe. The children scurried about helping with camp chores and tossing rocks into the creek. With longing I watched the dimples in the pool that revealed feeding grayling. I had no fishing license; and even if I had, I doubt that I could have found my fly rod in the tangle of gear we hauled in the station wagon.

Someday I am going to plan a trip and leave home all unnecessary paraphernalia! Selecting only essential equipment baffles most campers, so we'll take a look at that subject in the next chapter to see if we can spare you some misery. But first you must decide how you will travel and what type of camp you want.

Of course, you can stay in motels or cabins. There is nothing wrong with that. As I mentioned earlier, if you are just going from here to there and back, there is not much money saved by pulling a travel trailer or driving a gas-gobbling mobile home. But if pleasure is your goal and you plan a leisurely pace, a camping rig is for you.

There are four main options in travel camping shelter: camper trailer, travel trailer, self-propelled rig, and tent. For the moment we will overlook those clever patented rooftop contraptions so wondrous to behold.

THE RECREATION VEHICLE BOOM

The variety and price range of recreation vehicles on the market today baffle the beginning camper. What should he buy? I urge him to search carefully and try several before making a decision. Most types of recreational vehicles can be rented at reasonable rates. Many happy family campers never plan to purchase their own. They find it more convenient and economical to rent a trailer for the few yearly opportunities they have for camping.

The lowest-priced rigs are the camper trailers, those fold-down canvas or fiber glass outfits seen scurrying about any roadway on a holiday. The careful shopper may find a satisfying secondhand trailer, but he should inspect it thoroughly, including the wheel bearings, canvas, and framing.

In addition to a lower initial cost, the camper trailer offers several advantages. The low profile on the road reduces towing costs, and usually no special equipment is required for the tow car other than a ball hitch and a hookup for lights. Insurance and depreciation costs are less; tires and maintenance are lower too. Properly cared for, a camper trailer wears well.

The camper trailer usually provides one double bed on either extended side, with space between for additional cots. During daytime hours, the space between the beds accommodates camping gear. Some offer built-in stoves, refrigerators, and other assorted conveniences. As options are added, the price approaches that of the camper trailer's bigger brother, the travel trailer.

When everything is working properly, a camper trailer can be readied for sleeping as quickly as any rig on the road. For the occasional family camper, or those who enjoy a modification of the tent camping experience, the camper trailer has much to recommend it. Newer, more expensive models equal the smaller travel campers in features and convenience.

THE TRAVEL TRAILER

The travel trailer is a mini-mobile home, and some of them are not so mini! Costs range up to the high priced trailer at thousands of dollars. Some provide only a shell for sleeping. Others amount to a modern home on wheels, complete with kitchen, living space, bedroom, bathroom, furnace, and air conditioning.

With care a quality model will last many years. The so-called bargain models shake apart rapidly. Careful maintenance insures safe travel and longevity, but you must equip your tow vehicle adequately to handle the weight and towing specifications.

Hauling a trailer cuts deeply into your gas mileage, and there is no way around it. When we calculated the cost of pulling our light, sixteen-foot travel trailer from Alaska on our fifteen-thousand-mile jaunt, we discovered we could have stayed in motels and picnicked along the way for an equal sum. (The cost included two or three tires that blew and a fifty dollar repair job in White Horse.) You can also expect your gas mileage to drop 35 percent to 50 percent when you hook on your travel trailer.

However, you do gain value when you locate in one spot for several days and pay trailer park fees rather than motel bills. You also gain in that you can stay reasonably close to any point of interest you choose. Many public campsites are still free, and few private sites will cost more than five dollars per day, including power, water, and sewer hookups. The price is certain to increase as the demand for space mounts.

Careful shopping can secure good used trailers at reasonable prices, though one must inspect the vehicle with care prior to purchase. Note the tires and brakes. Check the frame and undercarriage. Insist that the lighting be connected for inspection. Check whether the appliances are still functioning. Beware of gas furnaces in older models, for some families have lost their lives through improperly vented heaters.

The driver's attitude toward pulling a trailer should be determined through experience. Some people find a trailer intolerable. Some braking systems are automatic; others require coordination of a hand brake with the auto brakes. There should be no sway or weaving and no uncomfortable bouncing. If this occurs, either the trailer is improperly loaded, the hitch requires adjustment, or the trailer is poorly constructed. Never sign a contract for a trailer without first towing it behind a vehicle similar to the one you plan to use.

In any recreation vehicle, test your family's capacity to be comfortable. Sit in it as you would when eating. Lie on the beds. A child or adult may discover claustrophobia for the first time in the upper bunk of a camper. Make sure the ventilating fans exhaust cooking fumes and heat. Check water pressure systems and waste-holding tanks.

The rent-and-try rule pertains to all recreation vehicles, especially one that involves a significant investment. It is always cheaper to rent for two weeks a year than to own a vehicle if no additional use is made of it. Several books and magazines for the prospective travel trailer owner can be secured, describing values to look for and cautions when purchasing a recreation vehicle.

SELF-PROPELLED CAMPERS

The self-propelled camper completes the recreation vehicle family. Again, the variety seems endless. Van conversions account for many in this class; they are amazingly compact homes on wheels. The pickup camper is little more than a travel trailer mounted on a truck, either directly on the frame or within the box. At this writing, pickup campers and travel vans are under scrutiny by government safety authorities. No doubt design changes will be required, increasing both the safety and the cost of these vehicles.

The motor home is classed by many as the deluxe family camping vehicle, and perhaps this is true. Prices begin at the upper range of travel trailers and go up into the stratosphere. The appointments and options parallel those of the better travel trailers. The chief disadvantage is the high cost of operation and the lack of a separate vehicle once you reach your destination. This has led some to install a hitch and haul a light car along!

Van conversions are miniature motor homes. Some of

these amazing compact outfits work well for the smaller family. During fair weather which permits outdoor living, the van conversion is most enjoyable. The van offers relaxed camping for the family that does not enjoy pulling a trailer, though some inconvenience is found at the camp site since no separate vehicle is available.

In the early 1970s a modification of the pickup camper appeared, described as a "fifth wheel" camper. This unit mounts in the bed of the tow truck much like a semitrailer attaches to its tractor, providing the advantages of the trailer but with a more stable towing capability. The camper can be detached quite handily, freeing the pickup for use away from camp.

You can spend from four to five hundred dollars on your recreation vehicle, or you can spend twenty thousand. Your sense of stewardship, economic level, and family interests will guide you in making a purchase decision. I urge you to buy with care. Rent a variety of vehicles before buying, and you will be more likely to find satisfaction.

But you can enjoy all the benefits of travel camping without spending a lot of money. Your present car will do, and your basement and attic already contain much of the gear you will need.

ANYONE FOR TENTS?

With proper equipment and adequate preparation, tent camping allows you to take your family camping at a cost scarcely higher than staying home. You can load everything on your car, if you plan well, or haul a light utility trailer, if your family is large. A very adequate tent for a family of six can be purchased for less than one hundred dollars.

You will have to shop around before deciding which tent will be best for you. The simpler the construction, the longer it will last. Avoid buying low-budget models because their they will not last many seasons. Some version of the umbrella tent with an exterior frame will perhaps serve you best. But you will find cabin tents, schooner tents, pneumatic tents, and many hybrids. Visit a dealer and inspect his display. Select one that provides the floor space and head room you need for comfortable family enjoyment. You will want a shelter fly too, but more about that later.

Some tents include privacy curtains on side rooms for growing families, but consider also the possibility of a second lightweight tent for the older youngsters. They like to sleep alone, and you will have an auxiliary tent for side trips.

Avoid the coated nylon tents for auto camping. Though they are tough and attractive, most of them sweat miserably from the breathing of several sleeping campers. Nylon has its place, especially for trail camping, but neither bulk nor weight is the determining factor in choosing your family camping tent.

A variety of tent fabrics with mysterious names can be found on the market. The most common material is simply high-count cotton. Be sure all seams are reinforced, as well as all ties. Low-priced, bargain tents are usually inadequate. Occasionally you may find a closeout sale or a source for factory seconds which will serve, but you are not really saving if you skimp on your tent.

Be sure the tent is big enough. Someday the rain will

fall, and you will be amazed at how a tent seems to shrink as the day wears on and the children grow restless! The tent should have a sewn-in floor, rain flies that operate from the inside (though some excellent tents violate this principle), high quality zipper closures, mosquito netting, and plenty of ventilation.

If you have doubts about the size tent to buy, lay out your family sleeping bags on the living room floor and measure the square feet required. Add 50 percent and purchase a tent with that much floor space or the next larger size.

Check the quality of the metal framing. Thin-walled tubing is certain to twist or break. Complicated, ingenius designs may never be assembled properly, even with the instructions! All hardware should bear the mark of good engineering. The tent is your most costly piece of equipment. Buy from a reputable dealer on the advice of experienced campers.

A tent camper needs a rain fly, which also doubles as a sunshade. This calls for additional poles and lines, but it is worth it. If your campsite permits, erect your fly immediately in front of the tent, to allow the family to move in and out without getting wet and tracking dirt into the tent. In fair weather you may wish to place the fly away from the tent for more ready access.

A floor cover inside the tent door will save hours of cleaning. Plastic will do in an emergency, but its slippery surface renders it less suitable than a light rug or square of tent cloth.

Probably you already know that tents have limitations in foul weather, no matter what the advertiser claims. Most new tents leak until they have been soaked. Hose down a new tent prior to your trip. Some tents persist in leaking along the seams, where the stretching opens small holes at each thread. Waterproofing sticks are available to correct this, and waterproofing spray cans will help maintain a tight tent, year after year.

Warn your family not to rest anything against the tent during a rain. Any object pressed against the fabric sets up capillary action introducing a trickle of water at that spot. Once the tent dries, the leak disappears. Another common source of trouble is bug spray. Never spray directly on the tent. This destroys the seal, and the tent must be waterproofed again.

Guard the tent from campfire sparks and sharp objects. Never pack tent stakes in with the tent, and be sure the tent is dry before packing. If it is necessary to transport a wet tent, bundle it loosely and expose it to air as soon as possible to avoid mildew. Practice pitching your new tent at home, marking jointed poles for easy assembly at camp. Many families who could afford any kind of vehicle they desire still camp with a tent, because they perfer it that way.

4

Family Camping Equipment

HAVING LOOKED at the choices in travel and shelter for the family as they camp, the next consideration is basic equipment needs for comfortable outdoor living. The variety and price range are so vast that you must study your needs carefully. Talk with experienced campers and visit camping shops. My prejudices in certain areas will be obvious, and contrary to the opinion of other campers. Often the choice must be made on the basis of taste rather than utility. But buy good quality, even though you may not plan to camp extensively. Cheap is not inexpensive when it comes to camping gear.

Obviously your choice of gear will differ according to the type of camping you plan to enjoy. Backpacking demands minimum gear, the canoe trip with short portages allows slightly more, the pack animal trip more yet, and auto camping tempts the family to empty the house.

As you gain experience, you will discover how simple life can become; and you will learn how dependent we are on frills and gadgets! Impulse packing inevitably clutters a trip, often causing some essentials to be forgotten. Carefully planned, disciplined selection of personal and camping gear brightens your camping day before it begins.

A Good Night's Sleep

Two of the most important dimensions of family camping are eating and sleeping. Without satisfying meals and ample rest, nothing else will count for much.

Camping vehicles can accommodate the sheets and blankets from home, but this only complicates camp life. The sleeping bag offers the most practical answer to the bedding problem.

What kind of sleeping bag should you choose? The Dacron filled bag seems to serve best in the moderate price line. No doubt other synthetic fillers bearing other trade names will do as well. The bag should contain at least three pounds of filler, unless you live in a hot climate. Warmer bags are not ordinarily needed for the typical family camp, and a spare blanket is a happier solution than a bulky sleeping bag that proves too warm for most nights.

If you plan frequent pack trips, the down-filled bags are worth the added cost. Again, choose a bag that suits your average need. Should you wish to camp in colder weather, carry a down liner or buy down-filled underwear for pajamas.

Speaking of pajamas, the best I have found is a pair of loose-fitting cotton pants and an equally loose-fitting hooded sweatshirt. In extremely mild weather, the sweatshirt may be replaced with a T-shirt. With this attire, getting up is less traumatic on a cool morning. You are already respectably dressed, and you can tend to early morning chores by adding only moccasins or sneakers. When the camp is under control, you can change to your regular clothes. This plan works equally well for the ladies.

The hooded sweatshirt is important because the head accounts for much of the heat loss that makes for cold sleeping. My other warming trick calls for a pair of wool socks reserved for sleeping. I leave mine in the sleeping bag. Never go to bed wearing damp socks. Tuck them into the sleeping bag, and they will be dry in the morning.

When you are camping by auto, you probably will find sufficient space to haul camp cots, at least for the adults. They are worth the space and effort. We use foam pads on the cots and sleep as comfortably as we do at home. For the children, foam pads on the ground will do, if you have pitched your tent on a fairly level, rock-free spot.

To keep dampness from the floor, lay a plastic sheet under the tent floor. Be sure this does not extend beyond the perimeter of the tent, for rain will run down the tent sides and collect on top of the plastic, soaking the floor instantly. Some argue against plastic if the tent is to be left standing for a considerable time, but I am not convinced by their arguments. A good trick for any tent that remains in one spot for several days is occasionally to place several blocks under the floor to allow air to circulate, making the tent more pleasant.

One more tip for comfortable sleeping. I have carried a plastic tarpaulin with ties attached so that I can cover my tent when rain threatens. The tent is reasonably waterproof, but it is much more pleasant to pack a dry tent. Your tent design may prohibit this, but I have found it helpful.

I have given up air mattresses in favor of foam pads. Pads never go flat in the middle of the night. They do not require inflation. They weigh less than air mattresses, though they appear more bulky. I cannot cite engineering studies, but I believe you will find an inch-and-a-half of foam to be more effective insulation than a properly inflated air mattress. If you do use an air mattress, be certain that it contains only enough air to barely keep you off the ground. When you sit up, you should feel the ground. Cots with foam pads, though, insure good sleeping. On the trail, just carry the pad. Pillows are an option you can wrestle with. If there is room, why not?

The question of heating tents and trailers must be considered with extreme care. A properly designed furnace system takes care of travel trailers and mobile homes. Several firms manufacture catalytic heaters using white gas or propane for fuel. These are efficient, but adequate ventilation *must* be provided. While they are relatively fumeless, they burn sizeable quantities of oxygen. Never employ charcoal for heating purposes, or cook with charcoal inside unless a well-ventilated fireplace is used. Charcoal gives off carbon monoxide, as well as burning oxygen. All heating systems should be inspected regularly to assure safe operation.

THE CAMP COOK

Camp cooking differs little from home cooking, except, hopefully, Dad lends a hand. You can cook almost anything in camp you would serve at home, providing you bring along the right gear. Not too many campers attempt fancy baking, though this is possible too.

The source of heat must be decided. Open fires are romantic, but a nuisance for cooking, and they are being banned more and more by public and private camps. In some areas firewood is unavailable. Charcoal is a viable option, but it is messy and slow unless you invest in one of those quickie patented charcoal starting rigs. The best solution for day-by-day auto camp cooking seems to be the LP gas stove.

Those who camp with recreation vehicles usually have a built-in stove. Others can buy a two-or three-burner model for a reasonable price. The trend seems to be away from the pressure gasoline models, even though they provide excellent heat if handled properly. Serious accidents have resulted from carelessness or ignorance. White gas is treacherously volatile.

The most economical method is the LP gas stove with a refillable gas supply. The small throw-away cylinders serve well, but they increase the cost and they always seem to run out in mid-oatmeal, just when you remember you forgot to get a spare cylinder. When camping in the mountains, expect a decrease in the heat output of your LP stove.

Recreation vehicle owners soon build an efficient collection of cooking gear, but tent campers must work at it a bit more. A plywood camp box designed to hold your basic cooking equipment will prove valuable. You can buy pre-cut models to assemble at home, or you can design your own. An assortment of cardboard boxes is less than satisfactory.

Nesting camp cook kits serve well, though you will need a supplementary griddle or fry pan. When you cook over charcoal or an open fire, be sure to soap the exterior of every pot. You will find the soot will rinse off easily when cooking chores are done.

Many camping parks provide a picnic table at each site,

and travel campers have tables inside. But tent campers may want to purchase a light folding table and camp stools. A couple of folding lawn chairs feel great at day's end too, especially when you plan to spend several days at one spot.

While the traveling camper will want to plan menus in advance, food may be purchased along the way rather than hauling a stock of groceries from home. Ice is readily available in most places for the cooler, but it is more practical to purchase milk and meats each day.

Food preparation becomes a bit more complex for the family traveling through the wilderness, and we will discuss menus for trail camping in greater detail later on. We will deal with the selection and packing of personal gear at that time as well, for often a trip will blend the auto camp with side trips into wilderness areas.

To Rent or to Buy?

Christian stewardship requires that we carefully weigh the investment a family makes in every area of life. Some families with limited time or funds may decide they cannot take up camping. Other families may desire to enjoy some camping, but other interests have priority for time and money. These families should investigate rental opportunities for both vehicles and equipment.

The family camping boom has given rise to a broadening rental industry. It is now possible to rent a complete outfit at rates compatible with most family budgets. If only one or two weeks of camping per year is anticipated, renting equipment is almost certain to be the most economical route to take. Rates and kinds of equipment available for rent vary greatly in different sections of the country.

The most extensive and competitive—thus the most reasonably priced—outfitting services in the world can be found in the Minnesota Boundary Waters Canoe Area with the principal businesses located in Grand Marais and Ely. Here you can outfit your family for from three days to a whole season of wilderness camping for as little as $11 per person per day, and less for the children. Your outfit will include canoes, food and all camping gear, everything except your personal effects. Even sleeping bags and pads are provided by most outfitters.

At this writing, several Christian camps are experimenting with outfitting services for families. More will undoubtedly add this ministry to their program, opening wilderness vacations to more families. Addresses for securing information on Christian camping wilderness programs are listed in the sources of information at the end of this book.

PLANNING AND PACKING

Our concluding chapter will deal with plans for next year's trip, but right now we will discuss the trip immediately before you. Get out your pencil! Divide your packing into categories. What do you need for general camp chores? Cooking gear, food staples, first aid, et cetera. What about travel needs? Be sure to include such important items as maps, record book, credit cards, insurance identification, spare glasses, and key telephone numbers.

List all the equipment and supplies you feel you must have, then check off the items as you pack them. If in doubt, leave the item home. Do not overlook camera and film, binoculars, and games and other diversions for the children. Then draw up a personal list for each family member. A small bag marked with each person's name will simplify organization. Dress clothes, if needed, can be hung together in a garment bag.

Organize clothing and equipment carefully in your car or camper. The more simply you can travel, the happier everyone will be. Wash and wear clothes have proven a boon for campers. Almost all private camping parks offer laundromats.

Each family devises its own system for planning and packing; but leave nothing to chance. Write your list and check it off. Help the children compile their lists and teach them responsibility. One of the chief values of family camping lies in the many opportunities parents and children enjoy to work together. The trip begins at home!

TIPS FROM A PRO

Gil Faber, Trip Information Director for the National Campers and Hikers Association, issued a bulletin called *Tips on Travel Camping* with many helpful ideas for families just getting started. The remainder of this chapter is adapted from that bulletin.* The costs Faber lists need adjustment in some items for your vehicle may be more expensive to use and camping fees will probably average more too. The Fabers apparently based their figures strictly on tent camping.

* * *

Thirteen years ago the four of us packed our family

---

*Used by permission.

sedan with a collection of new and borrowed equipment and started out on our first camping trip. It was difficult getting to sleep the night before that first trip and now, 80,000 miles and many trips later, it is still just as exciting. We specialize in western trips but the following material applies to any part of the country.

PLANNING: THE MOST IMPORTANT INGREDIENT

If you have no worries about time or money, you are fortunate. Most of us, however, have limited budgets of both time and money for our vacations. And, naturally, we want to have an interesting and comfortable trip. So every trip is usually preceded by a planning period. In our family this is almost as much fun as the trip itself. Plan carefully for cost, time, interest and comfort.

Our basic formula goes something like this. Take a map of North America. Mark three circles on it, all centered on your home town. The smallest circle should have a radius of about 500 miles. The medium circle about 1,600 miles, and the largest about 3,000 miles. For those of you who are not scientists, the radius is the straight line distance from the center to the edge of a circle. Generally speaking, the average family with a desire to travel will find the following formula works out:

RADIUS	TIME	ROUND TRIP	COST
500 mi.	½ to 1 week	1000 mi.	$ 50
1600 mi.	2 to 3 weeks	3500 mi.	$150
3000 mi.	3 to 4 weeks	7000 mi.	$275

Plus entertainment, film, souvenirs, tools and food, which is the same at home.

An important point to remember is that the time can be extended considerably without increasing the "out of pocket" cost significantly. Each day extra in a state park adds only the overnight fee while the National Park and National Forest campgrounds are usually free in conjunction with the annual Golden Eagle sticker which can be purchased for ten dollars.

The cost of a trip depends on distance and days. Here is our cost formula, and just to show that it works, I have included the actual costs of three of our own trips:

How far you can travel in a day is an individual matter. Generally we plan to have an interesting, enjoyable day. We try to get most of our daily miles under our belt by early afternoon, before the late afternoon heat has started to wear on us. Frequent, short stops and visits to points of interest help to break up the monotony. And we like to have a few hours to explore or relax or perhaps go for a swim in our overnight park. By driving at maximum safe speeds permitted by law and our load, we can make from 350 to 450 miles a day. For a full day's travel we plan for a maximum of eleven to twelve hours on the road. At least two hours of this is for stops including breakfast, lunch, gas stops, and shopping. Here is our formula for average driving time:

Type of Road	Mph
Turnpikes and interstate highways	50-60
State highways:	
Plains states and West	45-50
Midwest	40-45
Populated East and West Coast	35-40
Mountain highways	25-35

ITEM	PLANNED COST	ACTUAL COST		
		Vt.-N.H.	Florida	West
		9 days 1600 mi.	14 days 3600 mi.	30 days 8300 mi.
Gas, oil, lubes	2¼¢ per mile	$ 35	$ 81	$188
Tires and repairs	¾¢ per mile (long trip)	..	..	63
Park and camp fees	$2.50 per day	20	30	30
Entertainment, film, etc.	Up to family	6	25	60
TOTAL COST		$ 61	$136	$341
Food and supplies	Same as at home	Same as at home	Same as at home	Same as at home
Saved on motels, restaurants, etc.	$15-$16 per day	$125	$200	$500

We enjoy rising and retiring with the sun when on the move. A typical day for us goes like this: Up at 4:30 A.M., leave camp at 5:15, breakfast at 7:30 in roadside park (Dad shaves while Mom fries the eggs and the kids stretch their legs because they have been napping until now, and so has Mom probably), gas stop at 10:00, lunch in roadside or town park at 12:00 noon, gas stop and shopping at 3:00 P.M., arrive at overnight at 4:00, supper at 5:00, swim or hike and relax around campfire until bed at 8:30. By planning this way there is always time for the unexpected stop for car repairs or extra time for exploring something special along the way.

NOW THAT WE KNOW HOW, LET'S PLAN A TRIP

Suppose we say we have a full three weeks (this means twenty-three days), a budget of about $250, and the old auto is in good shape. Our circles on the map tell us that we can pick out any destination in the 1,600 to 3,000 mile radius as long as we travel no more than 5,000 or 6,000 miles. We have been reading up all winter on the Western National Parks so we get out this year's *Rand McNally Road Atlas* and go to work! While developing the general plan we frequently consult our campground guide so we can select routes that will provide us with good overnights at the right spots. Our favorite is the *Rand McNally Campground Guide*.

After a lot of study and several family confabs, here is the result:

Destination	Miles Traveled	Days	
		En Route	There
Black Hills—Mt. Rushmore	1500	4	1
Cody, Wyoming	400	1	⎫
Yellowstone National Park	100		5
Grand Tetons National Park	50		⎭
Salt Lake City	300	1	1
Routt National Forest	300	1	
Rocky Mountain National Park	150	½	1½
Colorado Springs	150	½	1½
Home (Isn't it beautiful!)	1600	5	
Sightseeing allowance	4550 450 ——— 5000	13	10

By allowing five days for the trip home, we can include quite a bit of sightseeing or just plain loafing along the way. Or, if we overstay at any of the previous points, the last 1,600 miles could be covered in four or even three days.

Applying our formula, we find that this trip will cost about $150.00 for car expense (if we don't buy any tires, we can put the money away for them). The allowance of $2.50 per day for park and camping fees brings the total up to about $200.00, and we will have $50.00 for film, entertainment, tolls, etc. Rarely will we spend $2.50 per day for park and camping fees on a trip west, but we have found that some tenderfeet run for a motel at the slightest sign of rain.

SOME MISCELLANEOUS ADVICE

Here are many little bits of knowledge that will contribute to your comfort and ease of mind while traveling:

1. Use traveler's checks and oil company credit cards.
2. Leave a copy of your itinerary with family or close .friends.
3. State parks in populous areas are usually filled up by Friday at noon in season. Private campgrounds will be less crowded for your Friday and Saturday overnights.
4. National Park campgrounds fill up every day in season so schedule arrival before midafternoon. Morning arrival is best. If the park is near a large city, weekends are the same as state parks.
5. National Forest campsites in the sparsely populated areas of the West are usually not crowded. If near the highway, they may fill up late in the evening but there is usually room for more. These campsites are generally free and represent the ideal kind of camping we dream about. Dry toilets and no washrooms are the rule. Better facilities are usually coupled with a daily one-dollar fee or the annual Golden Eagle (ten dollars).
6. If heavily loaded in hot weather, use brakes sparingly, carry extra water, and try to schedule the bad mountain grades for the cool of the morning.
7. Do not carry large supplies of food. Shop daily and only stock up for several days when you are going to stay several days in a National Park or Forest where you cannot be sure of finding good stores.

8. Mountains and high altitudes can get very cold at night in midsummer. Carry medium or lightweight sleeping bags plus one sheet and one blanket per bed. In cold weather, sleeping on the ground is much warmer than on a cot without a pad.

9. Use layers of clothing—sport shirts, cotton slacks, one sweater, and one medium or heavyweight jacket will provide flexibility. Use seersucker and "wash and wear" cottons to minimize ironing.

10. Heavy-duty cartons are ideal for clothing and food boxes. They stack easily and are handier than suitcases and large chuck boxes.

11. Do not bother with a shelter fly and poles unless you have the space. We have rarely used ours while traveling. A one-gallon gas can is much better than the larger ones. A single mantle lantern occupies much less space than a double mantle and is just about as bright. Carry extra ropes or cord and a few pieces of plastic sheet for all-purpose covers.

12. A small hand axe and a twenty-inch bow-type pruning saw are all you need for cutting firewood. Keep the axe sharp and sheathed! Use it only for splitting or trimming.

13. Insect repellent is a must. Use it at the first sign of mosquitoes. Don't wait for a sign of chiggers, especially in the Midwest. If in grassy areas, put repellent on ankles, socks, and pant cuffs. The liquid repellent is the most economical and easiest to apply. Sticks and sprays are more expensive and hard to apply. Carry a bug bomb for bombing your tent when necessary. **Sandy** or **beach** areas may have armies

of ants. Any chlorinated cleanser sprinkled on the ground will turn back ants. If your outfit is not insect tight, use it at points of access such as trailer legs, etc.

14. When in very hot weather, keep your film under clothing or blankets to avoid high temperatures.

15. Watch your camera exposures in the West. Long-range mountain scenes require ½ stop less than normal. Desert scenes about full stop less (i.e., if normal is f 8 at 1/100, use f 11). A haze filter is a good investment for open shade and marine or mountain scenes. Consult your camera store for confirmation of this and other tips on photography.

16. Aluminum cups are not good for drinking hot liquids. Use them for soup or salads and get some plastic cups for coffee.

17. Pack top carrier as though wrapping a package by laying eight-foot-by-ten-foot tarp on bottom and fold-in from both sides then back to front and front to back. Use web straps. Mount carrier as far forward as possible to balance car load. There is an unexpected bonus in using a top carrier. It shades and insulates the car roof from the sun and with air space underneath this can mean as much as ten degrees cooler in the car on a hot day.

18. If you intend to camp frequently in cool weather, a catalytic tent heater is a good investment. Remember, however, that ventilation is necessary to replace the oxygen consumed by the heater. Carelessness can be fatal! This applies to the use of any heating or cooking equipment.

5

Camp Worship and Witness

WHEN WE CONSIDER family devotions on camping trips, we must go back to the home. Hitching the trailer to the car does not magically produce a devotional habit. But camping does provide the opportunity to give fresh thought to this often discussed but infrequently practiced matter.

Life in camp can be controlled through planning more readily than life at home. But unless devotions have been deliberately planned and designed to fit naturally into the day, they will be squeezed out or observed in a meaningless, perfunctory manner.

A happy solution to Sunday worship is a family visit to a nearby church where you meet new people and may come to a deeper appreciation of the church back home! But public worship in church does not resolve the issue of personal and family worship.

Is it possible that our powerful urge to attend church grows out of a sense of religious duty? We do not always evaluate what happened in church, whether we actually met God, or whether we helped anyone else. Just being in church fulfills a duty and we feel good.

How Much Is Spiritual?

This sense of urgency over religious patterns has spilled over into other areas. A few years ago I launched a series

61

of wilderness trips as an outreach for resident Bible camps. Some were suspicious of this innovation. They said, "I don't see how wilderness camping can offer much spiritual help. There's little time for Bible study."

Interestingly, this comment never came from a person who actually shared one of our trips. I have no doubt the comment was sincerely offered. Yet I cringe each time someone asks, "How much time do you devote to spiritual things out there?"

My reply is direct and simple. "Twenty-four hours a day." I dislike hearing the term *spiritual* used to define a category of activity, implying that all other activity is unspiritual, nonspiritual or something else. I much prefer the word *devotional* to distinguish Bible study and worship from the other aspects of camp life. Everything must be spiritual or it has no place in Christian camping.

The spiritual part of family camping is everything you do! Until you grasp that, meaningful worship is impossible. When we begin to live in constant wonder at the perpetual presence of Christ in our lives, worship will come alive for us and our families.

THE PLACE TO BEGIN

Family worship must begin with Mom and Dad on their knees in private. Worship ritual is comparatively easy to establish, and much that passes for family worship is only ritual. The worship that touches children's hearts is an overflow from the parents' hearts, and nothing else will do.

Consider what the Bible says about the ultimate in spiritual gifts. Read 1 Corinthians again. Patience, kindness, humility, forgiveness, acceptance, trust, politeness—all the other life qualities listed in this chapter—are not the result of being spiritual, they are the *essence* of spirituality. The highest expression of Christ's presence in your life is found here. No ritual can take its place.

I am not suggesting that you abandon times for prayer and Bible reading. I am hoping you will quit worrying about it, and treat family worship just as you treat other important elements in life. If you miss a meal, you do not stop eating. You are all the more ready when the next opportunity comes.

Let me call your mind back to childhood. How did the church service, religious ceremonies, sermons and all the patently adult-oriented practices we bundle together and call Christianity appear to you then? The finest aid to understanding your children is a good memory! Let me share my memories as a basis for considering family devotional life while camping.

A CHILD'S-EYE VIEW

I am fully persuaded that every home needs a church, and that all parents need help in raising their children. Family camping is one small portion of life and it has its limitations, both by reason of economics and wear and tear on the nervous system. The church fellowship supports parents in steering children into proper pathways. But my boyhood problem was this: none of the pathways my church steered me toward seemed particularly exciting, and almost everything that I felt was fun was frowned upon.

Bear in mind that we are discussing a child's viewpoint. Mature people suffer from no such ideas. But it seemed evident to my boyish mind that sermons were the chief preoccupation of the church (whether preacher sermons or Sunday school teacher sermons, or VBS leader sermons). The cardinal propositions of the gospel appeared to be: sit down, sit still, and listen. And there I was, possessed of a demon that urged me to stand up and make noise. I dearly longed for someone to listen to me. I never seriously considered rebelling, but it did occur to me that some reasonable diversions were in order, yea, inevitable; and those diversions occasioned much pain and woe, and a good deal of prayer among the deacons.

Then one summer day, as I rested on the old plank steps in front of our house, a most wonderful event occurred. A band of boys trooped up the sidewalk, bearing assorted burdens. A lumpy packsack, a hiking stave, a hatchet hung at the waist, and rope bound in official Scout fashion swinging from a belt clip. As the boys marched by, I heard one say, "We leave in the morning, eight o'clock, rain or shine!" A patrol of scouts from a neighboring church were bound for adventure which would take them into the woods *over Sunday*. I knew they could not possibly be Christians.

But they were boys! And I wanted to be one of them more than anything else in the world. I wore out two scout handbooks before I reached the age of twelve (as was required in those days) and was permitted to join the troop. This moment my eye falls on a cherished book on my shelf, a blue-bound edition of the Scout manual identical to that which I loved as a boy. You wonder why carnal anger arises when I visit a church and hear someone say, "Well, we'd like to do something for our boys, but we're too busy."

My scout days caused concern among the faithful in our home church, for our troop shared a wondrous cabin in the forest seven miles from town. Every fourth weekend was our troop's turn. The men who took us camping taught us the ways of the forests; taught us to chop wood and build fires, to use a compass and tie knots. To a boy, these are matters of importance. While winter howled outside our cabin, we shared the comradeship of men and boys. The lantern hissed and the great oil drum stove glowed cherry red. Gentle profanity rose when the card game went askew, and cigar smoke curled up toward our top bunk. There were stories I did not understand which seemed funny to the older boys, and on Sunday morning we sat in a circle and hurried through the Sunday school lesson leaflet.

Those good, dear men who taught me so much could not teach me about God, because they did not know Him. Some would say that my boyhood would have been more secure had I not been exposed to such men! I ask those people, why didn't a man from my good, gospel church come forward with equal adventure? The reasons seemed painfully clear. A good Christian has no time for fun, not if he is really serving the Lord.

That hardly seemed right to a boy.

You have your own reflections on the child's perspective, and you do violence to reason if you insist on a pattern for family worship that does not include the child's viewpoint.

A Pattern for Worship

What is worship? Some would define it as an awareness of God's loving presence, or praise and thanksgiving, an exultation of the heart that says with the psalmist, "Bless the Lord, O my soul: and all that is within me, bless his holy name" (Ps 103:1). But is worship only a brief euphoria?

When you plan family devotions, what do you expect will happen in your children's hearts? How can you focus everyone's thoughts on the Lord?

God visualized Himself for Israel through a pillar of cloud and fire. Everyone could see the symbol of God's presence and know He was still there. I believe God visualizes Himself for us, too. He gave us the Bible.

The relation between Bible study and worship is sometimes clouded. I am convinced they are the same. When we attend to His Word, and respond with our hearts, we are engaged in high worship. I will outline a pattern you may consider as you plan family worship for your camping trip.

As I worked on the program for our wilderness trips mentioned earlier, I wrestled with the matter of Bible study. I wanted more than a token study, and surely more than quickie homilies from myself and other leaders. The first trip offered an opportunity to experiment and the results were gratifying.

We planned a father-son trek in Wyoming's Bridger National Forest, basing at the Box Y Ranch. For a week we roamed the mountains on foot and on horseback. I chose six events from the life of Jesus which occurred on the mountains. Each story contained a wealth of teaching material, but I was determined not to lecture.

From each story I selected a theme verse to be our anchor point each day. The most difficult part of the plan lay in the leaders' compulsion to declare what God was saying. This is the normal approach to Bible teaching, but it was not appropriate to my experiment.

Each day was to contain three devotional periods. Occasionally the time was shifted, and a rain storm washed out one period entirely, but we accepted this without undue concern. We set no time bounds. We would quit when interest lagged.

The experiment began the first morning following breakfast. Everyone paused for Bible exploration. We asked two questions: What is God saying to us in this story? and What are the facts, and what do they suggest for the world today? We read from Matthew 4, the account of the Mount of Temptation. Our theme verse was, "Man shall not live by bread alone, but by every word that proceeds from the mouth of God" (Mt 4:4).

Obediently, the leader did not lecture. He gently prodded men and boys to participate through questions. Several times we recited the theme verse. Some good thoughts were expressed, and we shared a brief prayer. That session lasted about twenty minutes. Some would run more than an hour, with no one aware of it.

Lunchtime found us in the mountains. Our horses grazed while we ate sandwiches. Then each father and son sought a quiet place apart where they could share the second devotional period. I called it reflection time.

I sat with my sons under an aspen tree and heard them tell what they thought God was saying in the story of the day. The question for reflection time was this: What is God saying to *me?* What response should I make? As we shared, I became aware that I had not done much listening to my boys through the years. I had been too busy talking, directing and preaching. I learned some new ideas during those sharing times. Soon we prayed, and mounted our horses for more adventure. We had spent perhaps ten minutes reflecting on the Word, reinforcing the thoughts born in the morning and praising God for His faithfulness in keeping His promises.

It was evening when we rode into camp, tired from a long day. We dispatched supper eagerly and put the camp in order for the night. A huge fire drove back the darkness and the chilly evening breeze as we took our places on log seats and recounted the day's adventure. Our rancher host spun yarns about wolf hunting in the early days.

Campfires are for sharing, and so the question we asked was, "What happened today that you would like to share?" The responses were mixed—some funny, some serious. We repeated our theme verse, which was practically memorized by then. We recalled the event again when on another night, on another mountain, Jesus had been alone and hungry. We went to our tents with prayer and song echoing in our hearts, and I trusted the Author of the Word to continue to teach the men and boys.

In my experiment I wanted to find what men and boys might learn when they concentrated on a limited portion of Scripture for a whole day. I did not test them for content or memory work, but in the years that followed this camp and others, many letters and words of testimony have come reporting spiritual discoveries, sometimes made alone in the night.

THE MASTER ON THE MOUNTAINS

I have recorded the story sources and theme verses we used on our trip as an example for planning your family worship. Select passages your children will find interesting, and do not neglect familiar Bible stories! If your children are older, you might choose to study from one of Paul's brief letters throughout your camping trip.

Mountain of Temptation	Matthew 4:1-11
	Theme Verse: Matthew 4:4
Mountain of Instruction	Matthew 5:1-16
	Theme Verse: Matthew 4:16
Mountain of Appointment	Luke 6:12-16
	Theme Verse: Mark 3:14
Mountain of Provision	John 6:1-14
	Theme Verse: John 6:9
Mountain of Transfiguration	Mark 9:2-8
	Theme Verse: Mark 9:8
Mountain of Commissioning	Matthew 28:16-20
	Theme Verse: Matthew 28:19-20

Spiritual riches come to those who worship through meditation. Let the Bible be your pillar of cloud by day, and you will find God's light brightening the night.

When the family includes small children, the familiar Bible story books provide a fine resource for worship. This is legitimate worship, even for adults. Reflecting on God's dealings with Bible characters can teach us useful lessons even in our sophisticated society. There is no *right* way for family worship. The pattern that causes your family to sense God's presence is the right pattern for you.

Visiting a new church can be a highlight for your whole family as they enjoy a camping vacation. So often children spend their formative years among one group of Christians, with little opportunity to meet new friends. Your worship plans for family camping should include visits to churches near your camp.

Driving through Wyoming one July, my two sons and I paused in a bleak mining town for supper. Finding no public park, we halted near an abandoned building on a hill. In the distance we saw a low, white church with three or four cars in the parking lot. *A committee meeting*, I thought.

Our route carried us by the church as we drove on, and almost on impulse we stopped, partly to inquire about the nearest campsite, partly to meet fellow Christians in this out-of-the-way village.

We found a prayer meeting about to begin, and a warm invitation to join them. I did not confess my ministerial background, but I suggested that my son might sing. He brought his guitar from the van and brightened the brief service. Then we joined the people in a home where a young man was recovering from an accident.

The pastor insisted we spend the night in his home. We went on our way the next morning warmed by meeting new friends, and grateful for the opportunity to bring some cheer to a lonely parsonage.

PATTERNS FOR WITNESS

Sharing Christ with others should become as natural as worship in the life of a Christian. Just as the parents' day-by-day life becomes the fountain for family worship, the life quality forms the basis for witness.

Our travel trailer bears the decals of several associations; the Christian Family Camping Association, Christian Camping International, The Wilderness Society, the National Campers and Hikers Association and others. Yet I would hope that we need no decal to let neighbor campers know I am a conservationist and a Christian.

What does your campsite look like when you leave? How do you respond to small needs around you? What sounds flow from your camp when something goes wrong? These form the background for your direct Christian witness when you are out camping.

I am not sure if camping makes people friendly, or if only friendly people go camping, but I have rarely met a grouchy camper. You will find many opportunities for talking about the Christian faith as you and your family go camping.

Neighbors will note your lifestyle—grace before meals, times of devotions, the absence of bickering. If you invite them for evening coffee with treats for the children, they will be open to conversation about Christ.

Camping cannot make a witness out of the person who remains silent back home, for true witnessing is not so much a program as a way of life. As you grow in the constant awareness of Christ's presence, you will want to make plans to share Him with others.

Your plans may include selected tracts or booklets. The gospel deserves the best in graphic arts. Something about the gray, newsprint folder discourages me, but then I discover someone who found Christ through just such a tract! A poor witness is better than none! Several attractive vacation folders have been prepared for campers and more will follow. Christian camping fellowships often make these available.

When you camp near National Forests and Parks, you may find worship services already established. Lend your support to these. You may be able to organize such a program if your talents permit, or you might simply invite a few fellow campers to your camp for the evening, then tell them what Christ means to you.

Caution should be observed in picking up hitchhikers, just as you should be careful not to camp in out-of-the-way places. Tragedies have ensued when Christians, trying to be helpful, disregarded these cautions.

One effective witness approach is to plan a trip with another family. Perhaps you know a neighbor who enjoys camping, but who is not a Christian. Invite the family for a trip where you can build a friendship and share Christ's love.

Avoid careless witnessing, such as blaring religious music or random scattering of tracts, which look much like litter to the one who must pick them up. Never fix a sticker motto on someone else's property without permission, and never paint *Jesus Saves* on a rock unless it is on your own personal property.

Let your witness be positive and loving. Hostile words and criticism of the beliefs of others accomplishes nothing.

The world is full of people with hungry, lonely hearts. You will find many people ready to listen for each one who refuses when you come with a cheerful, open message of God's love. After all, a witness is simply a report of an experience. No one can gainsay your walk with the Lord.

6

The Family on the Wilderness Trail

ONE KIND OF CAMPING every family should consider is the wilderness trip. While you may not choose a week-long trek through the mountains, you should at least sample the trails that lead away from the asphalt.

The importance of wilderness camping lies not only in the pleasure of new challenge, but in the potential such a trip offers for enriching your children. I am deeply grateful for the blend of influences that gave me a love for the outdoors, for I would be much poorer without it. While I have no desire to live in a remote cabin permanently, I look forward eagerly to my brief stays out there where my home is in my pack.

No other kind of camping teaches initiative and self-reliance so effectively, and no other environment presents a richer opportunity for families to become acquainted.

We will look at wilderness camping for the family, for fathers and sons, and for husband and wife. I will begin with the men in the family, for I have seen what camping has done for my boys.

A Boy and a Mountain

I saw my son hike off one day with his sleeping bag tied to his pack. He headed up a high Alaskan mountain with

74

meager rations in his pockets and a camera around his neck. He grinned and waved and said he would be back by and by. A friend standing nearby said, "How can you let him go off alone like that? What if something happens?" I watched the boy disappear up the wooded trail and prayed that something indeed might happen. He was about eighteen at the time.

Camping is good because it leads to self-discovery, and a young man needs to discover himself. I knew this boy, for we had camped together. I knew he possessed skills beyond mine and had agility I had long since lost. I knew, too, that dangers existed, but the risk was far less in those mountains than those he faced as he walked to school.

I thought about a day perhaps ten years earlier when that same boy and I pitched a tent near a lake about two hundred miles from that mountain. It was an ordinary day for me, just an overnight with one of my boys. As we busied ourselves with routine chores Dave stopped. His face was marked with joy. "You know, Dad," he said, "this is the first time you and I have ever been alone . . . just you and me."

I walked to the lake to think that over. Was it possible? A boy of eight, and he had never had his dad to himself? I pondered my life as a pastor, so busy with other people. *Dedication* I think they call it.

There were other camping times and other adventures, for camping is but one kind of family fun. Each of our children endured struggles for self-discovery along the way. But when Dave hiked up the mountain I had not the slightest fear, and I prayed something might happen, for you can hear very well on a mountain when it is still. Remember Elijah?

BUILDING DREAMS

So often I see myself in my sons, and I think about the way men grow. Not too long ago I slipped away to visit the haunts of my boyhood. I wanted to see how the woods and hills looked from an adult perspective, for I remembered much about my dreams as a boy. The hills seemed lower and the distances much shorter, but the little creek still flowed, and I suppose it grows to a torrent in the spring, just like it used to.

I hunted out the place where the first wild flowers bloomed each year, the blue and yellow violets, the May flowers and trilliums, the marsh marigolds—cowslips, we called them—and the wild rose. My secret wild plum tree was gone, dead of old age, I presume. Both my tadpole pond and the spring halfway up the hill had dried up.

But my memories were fresh and flowing. What amazed me, as I thought back were the number of dreams from forty years ago and more that have been fulfilled. Without conscious plotting they came to pass. I have come to believe that one of our biggest jobs as parents is to sow the right dreams in our children.

Long before I dared admit it, I wanted to be a preacher. There were days when I sat on the south side of the hill overlooking the lake and dreamed of writing stories and books. I longed to visit Alaska, and prowl the mountains with my rifle in search of game. I wanted to own a fly rod and lure trout from the mountain streams.

They were not very sophisticated dreams. But each of

them came to pass. But who planted those dreams? My parents had a part, of course, and the men who led our scout troop, and the boys whose company I sought. I felt again the obligation I owed these people, and I renewed my commitment to God to do what I could to help other boys dream. Family camping will build dreams for your sons and daughters, and the best dreams are found along the wilderness trail.

Of course, all that I say about sons pertains equally to daughters, for we enjoyed a wonderful girl in our home. We visit her now as often as possible, though she and her family live in Alaska. Yet perhaps dads and sons represent a kind of need most often neglected, and wilderness camping provides a rich opportunity to fulfill this need.

DADS AND SONS ON THE TRAIL

I know a man who took each of his sons on a week-long canoe trip when the boy reached age twelve. The trip with his youngest son was unusually brief because a bear stole their food packs. But the trip that the youngster had looked forward to for six years had become a reality and that was what mattered most.

Often several fathers and sons will share a camping adventure. I have organized several trips of this nature, and I would recommend that you give thought to this. One summer nine pairs of dads and sons from our home church took a canoe trip, and the younger boys' eyes sparkle as they anticipate their turn.

Perhaps one of the finest father-son trips I have shared took place in the Cascades in northern Washington. The party totalled thirty, including my two youngest sons. We combined backpacking and a horse pack experience, half the party hiked in and the other half rode, bringing a string of pack mules which carried most of our gear.

We enjoyed perfect weather. Scores of brook trout surrendered to our lures. We also explored an old mine. Warm days yielded to the evening chill, making our campfires doubly appreciated. For devotional periods we followed the Bible study plan outlined earlier.

The week passed swiftly, and near the end, a lad suffered an accident. Though painful, his injury permitted him to remain with the camp. His father tenderly looked after him. The lad's testimony at our closing campfire spoke to every father. He said, "I couldn't sleep much last night. But I did a lot of thinking. I straightened some things out with the Lord. And one more thing. Until last night, I wasn't really sure my dad cared for me. But now I know."

I wondered how well I communicated love to my boys as they struggled with adolescence. The closeness camping requires might tell many boys that their dad really loves them.

HUSBAND AND WIFE OUT CAMPING

Trail camping is a rewarding adventure for husband and wife, either alone or with other couples. Though the trip must be paced to the capacity of whichever partner is least secure, a few well-planned days on the trail can enrich any marriage.

Several years ago Elsie and I shared a canoe trip with our pastor and his wife and one other couple. I confess the men engineered the time and place to coincide with the peak of spring trout fishing in Ontario. We drove to Minnesota, picked up our gear at Duane's Outfitters, and pushed off from Moose Lake heading for Canada. Progress was aided by a light outboard on a square stern which towed the other two canoes.

Warm sun and favorable winds made the first day delightful, but rain started falling as we pitched camp. The rain continued through the next day, rendering the three-quarter-mile portage more taxing than we cared for, but finally we reached our base camp on That Man Lake and pitched the tents. The sky grew darker and a stiff wind blew in off the lake. The temperature dropped into the low 40's.

That was the story for the next two days. We slipped away between squalls and caught a few walleyes, but the trout eluded us. Most of the time was spent keeping the fire burning, preparing meals and cheering up one another. The women huddled under ponchos, glad for the foresight that included insulated underwear in the packs! Our three small tents flapped in the wind.

The third night the rain stopped and snow fell! When we crawled out of our tents in the morning, the sky had cleared and the landscape was breathtaking. Each tree and rock was frosted with fresh snow that glistened in the sun. The snow retreated before the rising sun and we took to the lake in search of trout.

How often we have remembered that trip over our late-evening coffee. The adverse weather and cold have been forgotten. The long portage is now a matter of pride. The mark of a camper is his ability to keep comfortable regardless of wind and weather, and to remain cheerful at the same time.

Camping as husband and wife in the sunshine is fun, and even adversity has a peculiar kind of pleasure. There is something good about being together in God's great world where man has not spoiled the beauty, a goodness the whole family should taste.

THE WHOLE FAMILY

Camping along the wilderness trail with the entire family challenges a growing number of homes each year. A mistake some families make is to launch into too ambitious a venture without adequate preparation. There is no use pretending that difficulties do not exist. But this is the challenge of camping.

Do not wait too long to introduce children to trail camping. Begin with a day-long ride or hike or paddle. Then graduate to an easy overnight where basic skills can be practiced. Then take in gradually extended trips with more demanding trails. I suspect most young people who reject wilderness camping were improperly introduced to trail life, or maybe the introduction came too late.

How early should camping adventure begin? I took my grandchildren on their first trip when they were four. We enjoyed three days on an island in the canoe country. The party spanned four generations, from my father at seventy-two to his great grandchildren at four. In between were my sons, a son-in-law, and me. The little boys were fitted with small packs and miniature paddles. This was their trip, a first encounter with the wilderness. I suspect it will not be my last expedition with those lads!

The rule in all camping is to pace the program to the abilities of the weakest. When sufficient leadership is available, you can divide a group, providing more challenging activity for advanced campers, but it is cruel to force a youngster beyond his abilities.

Provide a happy experience for your children and they will look forward year by year to trips with Mom and Dad. If you are a novice, team up with an experienced camping family for a fellowship trip.

Explore the delight of trail camping through day-long hikes and overnights from your auto camp. Many private and public camps offer nature trails and hikes to points of interest. Perhaps you could find a hiking trail near your home with picnic facilities or camp sites for your use. You might even consider a backyard camp-out where you can figure out how that tent frame goes together!

7

Following Trails Through the Wilderness

FAMILY CAMPING in wilderness areas takes three basic forms. The backpack trip, the horseback trip, and the canoe trip. Each possesses its unique charm. Backpacking is the most versatile, with trails to be hiked in almost every section of the country. The horseback trips are pretty much confined to the West, though dude ranches are springing up in many areas, utilizing trails in public lands. The canoe trip is more available than many people realize, though the North country lakes and rivers are best known.

Whether walking, riding, or paddling, you will discover muscles you forgot. Pretrip conditioning will make your adventure more rewarding and far less painful. A medical checkup should be routine if you plan a strenuous trip. We will not spend much time discussing travel, for each form brings unique problems and opportunities.

The horseback trip, while perhaps appealing to children, is the most expensive. Many packers require an additional hand for each five or six horses or pack mules. Since horses eat all year around, even though they may work only a few weeks or months a year, the cost runs high. For the average family, a ranch vacation with trail rides is most practical, but the pack trip remains a delightful way to explore the wilderness.

CANOE CAMPING

Several areas in the U.S. and Canada offer excellent canoe routes for families. The canoe permits you to be less fussy about the weight of gear and foods, but care is still required, for most routes include at least one portage.

Portaging a canoe is not difficult. The yoke balances the craft comfortably on your shoulders, though by the first evening you will be glad the portaging is over for that day. A seventeen-foot aluminum canoe weighs about seventy-five pounds, less for the lightweights, heavier for some models. Fiber glass canoes of similar dimensions weigh about the same with most features equalling the aluminum variety.

You must stay away from white water until you are experienced, and you will *never* run rapids where the slightest doubt exists. Canoeing is safe and enjoyable if you observe the rules.

We came upon an unforgettable scene one summer. A young man stood waste-deep in swirling rapids trying to dislodge his overturned canoe from between two boulders. His gear floated down the stream, and some had sunk irretrievably to the bottom. The small outboard motor had been his undoing. Approaching the landing above the rapids, he cut the engine, but before he could retrieve his paddle from beneath the packs, the current swept him into the rapids.

The canoe overturned, spilling his wife and poodle into the froth. Fortunately, the stream was not deep, and dan-

ger to life was small, but the drenched dog howled from a
rock in midstream, and the wife howled from shore. I
never heard a man take such a scolding! I suspect the
remainder of the trip was quite uncomfortable.

In most canoe areas you will find outfitters eager to rent
you canoes and other gear, eliminating the need for personal investment as you sample the joys of canoe camping.

HIKING

The simplest, and in many ways most rewarding, means
of wilderness travel is hiking. Thousands of miles of
marked trails await the traveler. The Appalachian Trail
winds from Maine to Georgia, 2,050 miles along the ridges
of the East. The Pacific Crest Trail covers 2,000 miles
along western mountains. In between you can find all
types of hiking terrain with all degrees of challenge.

As you might suspect, the feet are the hiker's best
friends. One blister can destroy an otherwise sound man
on the trail. Choose your footgear well, and break it in
thoroughly before starting your hike. Again, the art of
backpacking involves too much for detailed reporting here,
but you will find good resources listed in the appendix.
Read them, and practice short hikes at home with your
pack on your back.

The frame-type pack is the only suitable means for hauling your gear on a hike. Each of the many pack styles
serves its purpose, but settle for nothing less than a properly fitted pack frame. Padded shoulder straps add comfort,
and a waist band distributes the weight between back and
hips.

Men should not ordinarily attempt to carry more than

thirty-five pounds for all-day packing, women should limit pack weight to about twenty-five pounds. The children will want to carry their share, with weights suited to strength.

You can buy a lightweight cook kit, or you can assemble your own by saving various-sized cans. The advantage of tin can cookery is simple. You throw them away at trip's end! And they cost nothing. If you are careful not to leave them untended over the fire, ordinary cans will serve as well as the commercial cook kits. The #10 can holds about a gallon, all you need for trail camping, with many smaller sizes that nest nicely.

The badge of the hiker is his cup hooked to his belt. I personally find that a nuisance and tuck my cup in a side pocket of my pack. Sometimes in the mountains I carry a folded paper cup in my back pocket. What I lose in sanitation I make up in convenience. I am getting too old to lie on my belly and drink from a stream as I once did.

One compromise you can make is in your choice of sleeping bag. Pound for pound, nothing beats goose down filler, but you must pay two or three times as much for a down bag as you would for one with synthetic fibers. If you plan many trips, the down bag will add to your camping pleasure. But their bulkier, somewhat heavier, and very much cheaper cousins will do.

I have already mentioned my preference for foam pads over air mattresses, and here the cost is about the same. Children often eschew any padding, but that may not be wise. The pad contributes as much to warmth as softness. More body heat is lost through the ground than into the air when no insulation is provided.

Plan your menu carefully. Backpacking allows for few frills. One-pot meals are preferable, with a smaller pot for the coffee if you mistrust the instant variety as I do. Concentrated high-calorie foods are available for noon meals, eliminating the need for cooking.

When you plan a mountain hike, study the route description to learn where firewood is available. In higher altitudes lightweight stoves are required. Several varieties can be purchased which burn petroleum or alcohol fuels. The old-fashioned canned heat stove with jellied alcohol is not to be scorned for short trips, either.

Regardless of the kind of trip you plan, rules for health and safety are much alike. Know your equipment and study your route. Topographical maps covering almost every foot of the country can be purchased, and you should understand how to use a compass.

While it is possible to get lost, it is almost impossible to stay lost if you keep your head. In most areas, the best rescue signal is a hugh, smoky, controlled fire. Wandering aimlessly in hope of finding your way is foolhardy. You burn up energy and diminish the chances for rescue. Very often a lost person wanders into an area already searched and is missed by the rescue team.

HAPPINESS IS A LIGHT PACK

Regardless of the terrain or mode of travel, trail camping happiness is a light pack. On the Cascade father-son trip mentioned earlier, I found my saddle horse preempted for pack duty, leaving me on foot.

So I elected to be last up the trail to make sure no one lagged. Our base camp lay nine miles away over Twisp

Pass, a mild 6,000-foot elevation, as I recall. The day was clear and I enjoyed poking along at my own pace.

About three or four miles up the trail I came upon three of our campers, a dad and two sons. The boys were perhaps nine and eleven, and they were tired, but not nearly as tired as Dad! He sprawled on the side of the trail and said, "This is ridiculous!" I looked at his pack and agreed.

I had cautioned the hikers to keep their packs light, not more than thirty-five pounds for the men and bigger boys, twenty-five pounds or less for the younger lads. I hefted the tired camper's pack. It must have approached fifty pounds with a pair of heavy boots dangling from the frame. I imagine his longest hike in recent years had extended only from the parking lot to his office.

In a moment of weakness I said, "Let me help you for a while." That recharged the man's batteries. In fact, that was the last I saw of him until we reached camp! I discovered I was not in much better shape than he was. A heavy pack takes all the joy out of hiking, so plan your gear carefully, and leave everything home you do not really need.

Clothes for the Trail Trotter

Novice campers almost always pack too many clothes. The auto camper soon discovers the value of simple living, with regular visits to the laundromat to wash his wash-and-wear garments. The trail camper should limit himself to two changes in addition to the clothes he wears. And he uses the laundromat of the trail, a sturdy plastic bag. A few drops of soap, water from the stream of lake, and vigorous shaking accomplishes wonders for trail-soiled clothes. And who says one must don clean clothes every day? The hard-core light-pack camper takes one change of clothes and sometimes brings them home unworn!

Several layers of clothing provide greater comfort than bulky sweaters or jackets. A windbreaker, wool sweater, flannel shirt and warm undershirt will conquer even unseasonable weather in the summer. Of course, winter camping calls for another strategy.

An added word about foot gear is in order. Wear sturdy, well-fitting boots to protect the ankle and arch and *break them in before the trip!* In spite of repeated cautions, almost every group has at least one camper sporting brand-new boots, shiny and stiff. Blisters are inevitable! More than one camper has been forced to abandon a trip the first day out because he did not properly break in his boots.

The quickest and best way to insure foot comfort is to put your new boots on at home. Soak your feet (with the boots on) in the bathtub for ten minutes or so, until they are thoroughly wet. Then hike until they are dry! Someone is sure to scoff at this, but they have probably never tried it. Water does not harm leather if you do not attempt to dry it with intense heat. Never prop your boots near the fire to dry. They are sure to shrink.

Avoid wearing boots and overshoes of any man-made material on the trail. None of them breathe, and your feet will soon perspire and grow uncomfortable. Wear a light pair of socks, perhaps nylon, next to your feet, with a medium-weight wool sock. Rinse out the socks each night, wearing your extra pairs the following day. Comfortable feet make for happy camping.

A hat is important to shade you from the sun and to protect your head from insects. An old felt hat is excellent. Buying a fancy cowboy hat is a mistake unless you wear it long enough to feel comfortable. The bulk and broad brim, though romantic looking, are difficult to get used to. Nothing beats the broad-brimmed western hat if you can forget you are wearing it, but break it in, just like your boots.

Rain gear is essential on any extended trip. The poncho has many uses, but protecting a hiker from rain is not one of them. It does fit over a pack, but a lightweight nylon pack cover does the job better. Secure a waist-length, loose-fitting nylon rain jacket. Plastic jackets are a waste of money because they will rip quickly and prove useless. Do not worry if your legs get wet. They will dry. And if you are wearing wool pants, they will keep you reasonably warm even when wet.

Shorts can be worn at times, but not when the bugs are active, or when hiking through rough country. Long sleeves are recommended for protection, too. Carry at least one long-sleeved shirt in addition to your wind breaker.

One traditional western item you will find useful is the bandana. The western jeans are fine too, if washed two or three times prior to the trip to soften the material. Dress comfortably and sensibly. And keep your clothes sack small!

HELP FOR THE NOVICE

If you have had no experience camping in the wilderness, invite a veteran camping family to join you for your first trip. While reading books and magazine articles will prove helpful, you will learn best by observing an experienced camper.

Family camping clinics have been developed in several trips. Information about these clinics can be obtained by areas to provide basic training through actual short-term writing to Christian Camping International, Box 400, Somonauk, Ill. 60052. The clinics are conducted by Christian camps in several parts of the country, usually on a spring or autumn weekend.

The bibliography lists resources for learning about camping, associations for camping fellowship, and sources for camping equipment. Outdoor gear shops can be found in most communities where you can examine equipment. You will discover a wide variety of tastes and opinions among campers as to the best way to camp. The right way is the way that works for you and provides the adventure you seek on the trail.

GUIDELINES FOR PLANNING

How much gear is too much? Anything you can get along without should be left at home or in the car. Careful work with one camera lens will compensate for the heavy photo bag left behind. Four or five most effective lures in a pocket-size tackle box makes the multi-tiered fisherman's delight unecessary. Radios, hair curlers, shoe polish, cosmetics, and firearms do not belong in your pack.

Plan before you pack. Organize your gear into categories and assemble it in one place before beginning to stuff it into the packs. Here are suggestions to help you draw up your personal packing list. You must ruthlessly cut the list, or spend days on the trail regretting it.

CAMPING

Tent: stakes and poles if regulations prohibit cutting them along the way (green shrubs and trees may *never* be used for this purpose); rain tarp, if your tent requires one. *Tools:* Saw or light axe (axe not usually needed if a substitute is provided for driving stakes); sturdy pocket knife or sheath knife; tent repair kit; pliers, screw driver, an extra spark plug, and box of sheer pins if involved with outboard motors on the trip. A folding shovel is useful if latrines must be dug. It is not to be used for digging fire holes, which are a waste of time, or ditching tents, a violation of the wilderness ethic. Pitch the tent where the rain cannot run underneath, or construct a log dam on the uphill side from a fallen tree trunk. *Rope:* Light nylon line is excellent and inexpensive. *Plastic sheeting, 8' x 10'.* Useful for rain cover over firewood, gear, or tent; also as a wind shelter.

COOKING

Cook Kit: one of the nesting variety; an aluminum griddle, unless on a backpack trip where every ounce is counted; enough plates, cups, and silverware for the party; cooking utensils—large spoon, spatula, filet knife; old glove for working around fire; a cup-size throw-away plastic container for desserts, soups, etc. (wash and reuse throughout the trip); ample supply of matches in moisture-proof container (double plastic sandwich bag will do); fire grate. *Cleanup:* Detergent (biodegradable); scouring pads; roll of paper toweling for draining dishes; knit cotton or nylon sack for dipping dishes (allows boiling, but beware of boiling some plastics).

PERSONAL GEAR

CLOTHING: Two extra changes (wash clothes as needed); windbreaker; sweater; long-sleeve shirt; long pants; shorts (for warm, bugless days on clear trail); hat; comfortable hiking boots; loafers or sneakers for camp wear; wool socks; rain gear (light nylon, loose fitting). A poncho is of value, but not much good to keep person dry. Pack each person's clothes in a plastic or rubberized bag with name displayed.

SLEEPING BAG: Three-pound Dacron filler adequate for most summer trips; extra blanket for cold weather; foam pad, 48-inch length adequate; air mattress if you choose, but bring patch kit. Ground cloth under tent contributes to comfort. Use rolled-up sweater for pillow, or life vest if traveling by boat or canoe.

PERSONAL EFFECTS: Chapstick; sun lotion; glasses holder (elastic band around head); extra glasses; medications and personal hygiene needs; toothbrush; towel and soap; razor (if needed); sleeping clothes or pajamas; mosquito lotion; nonpolluting bug spray; toilet paper.

MISCELLANEOUS: Camera and film; binoculars; sewing kit (needles, nylon thread, buttons, safety pins, razor blade or small scissors); first aid kit (antiseptic, elastic bandage, gauze, Band-Aids, tweezers, burn ointment, laxative, Kaopectate, aspirin, compact first aid manual, fever thermometer, baking soda, long-nosed pliers if on fishing trip; flashlight; spare batteries and bulb; maps (protected in plastic from rain); compass; trail guides; emergency match supply.

FOODS

Because the selection and preparation of meals is so large a part of trail camping, a special section will be devoted to this. When backpacking, food packets will be distributed among all the hikers. Canoe and pack animal trips ordinarily include special food packs.

Organizing the Packs

Having assembled everything for the packs, plan carefully to keep handy those items most frequently used along the trail. Try to repack the same way each time, and soon you will find it easy to locate sweaters, rain gear, maps, rope, the noon lunch—saving much time and nervous energy as small emergencies arise.

Secure your compass to your belt with a line, or buy a wrist or pin-on model. Practice orienting your map with the compass, and always note the general lay of the land and your planned direction of travel. Advance thinking on these matters must be part of your trip planning.

Fit each pack to the family member who is to carry it and practice hiking with packs in place. Selective packing comes only with experience. In spite of great care, almost every camper finds he has carried much more than he actually needed. Evaluate your gear following every outing. Determine how frequently each item was used, and what substitute might have been employed. Make notes to discipline yourself the next time you pack. Beware of impulse packing, the random item you think might come in handy might be a bothersome extra.

Remember the limits: thirty-five pounds for men, twenty-five for women, twenty-five or less for children depending on age and development. Sure, you can carry more. But at day's end you will wish you had left some of it behind.

Create your own packing system. Do not trust your memory. Write down your list and stick to it. The obvious item often stays home because everyone assumed the other person remembered.

8

Comforts and Cautions on the Trail

AN INCREDIBLY FEW YEARS AGO wilderness living was the normal pattern for our forefathers. When you visit a restored old settler's cabin, you will be impressed that the pioneer had made peace with his environment. He lived from the forest and fields, bending with each season. He felt the wilderness to be inexhaustible.

He gave no thought to sleeping out under the sky or perhaps building a brush shelter. He cooked his fish and game over coals, found his way through unmapped wilderness, and kept a wary eye out for enemies, animal or human. (Though he faced no danger to match our freeways!)

Before him the Indian owned the land. He owned it for generations before arrogant white men stole it. The Indian knew a hard life, but what life he enjoyed came from the wilderness. He would smile at some of the fears novice campers bring to their camps.

Today we turn our backs on the city to seek a wilderness retreat. Each year it becomes harder to find solitude, and unless those who use the wilderness change their attitude, we will be the last generation to have a wilderness.

FEEDING THE FAMILY

Trail cooking can be as simple or fancy as you choose, but remember that fancy cooking takes time. Most backpack meals should be the one-pot variety, for your cooking gear will be limited. Reflector ovens or the aluminum Dutch ovens make campfire baking feasible, but breads can be prepared in simpler ways.

Techniques for cooking over an open fire demand more space than we can allow here, so I refer you to the books listed in the bibliography and I urge you to practice at home! Build a fire in the outdoor grill to learn how to control the heat by the use of small limbs or finely-split wood.

Once you learn to manage your cooking fire, you can qualify as an expert camp chef, for the major difference between home and camp cooking is the source of heat. The rule for the cooking fire is this: the least fire possible to do the job. Where hardwoods are available, your problem is simplified: build a bed of coals that give off steady heat throughout meal preparation. But most wilderness in the North offers mainly soft woods—cedar, pine, spruce or fir. These, along with aspen and birch, disappear in light ash with only brief life as coals. You must feed the fire with fresh wood constantly.

Take enough time to build a secure base for your cooking pots. Never place them directly on the fire, though the right size logs placed parallel can be employed when you have gained experience. A good solution for this problem is a portable grate which you level on a stone fireplace. Some campsites provide cooking grills built by the forestry service.

Firewood can usually be found with no trouble if you

hike a hundred yards or so from camp. My practice while canoe camping is to paddle down the shore away from the camp, then walk into the woods out of sight from the lake to preserve the integrity of the shoreline. I have never failed to find all the firewood I could use, and tent poles as well, with far less effort than gleaning the area adjacent to the camp which every camper explores.

When firewood is discussed, the camp axe comes to mind. The axe tradition dies hard, but you do not really need one. Carry a mallet for driving tent stakes and a bow saw, those marvelous tools with tough blades that will cut more wood with less effort than any axe ever invented. Under certain conditions the axe is invaluable, but camping families can remove one of the major sources of accidents if they leave the axe at home. A hand axe can be more dangerous than the long-handled variety.

Securing firewood can present a serious problem in the high country. And in some areas, open fires may be prohibited during fire hazard periods. Determine this prior to embarking on your trip and provide alternatives for cooking. Several lightweight camp stoves burning gasoline, kerosene or alcohol can be purchased. If the trip is brief and the weight is not a problem, a sack of charcoal will do. (Most campers use entirely too much charcoal when cooking.) But when conditions permit, the smell of coffee simmering alongside of a pan of frying fish over an open fire makes camping worthwhile all by itself.

TRAIL CAMP MENU

Feeding the family away from the supermarket is not as difficult as you might think. Several firms stand ready to serve you with complete menus packaged for two, four, or six persons. Packets are complete right down to measuring bags and scouring pads for cleanup. There are no problems of refrigeration, trash disposal or breakage.

If you have not tried dehydrated and freeze-dried foods for several years, you are in for a happy surprise. The taste and ease of preparation has improved greatly. The variety of camping meals has broadened from the days of canned beans to include scrambled eggs, cocoa, pudding, macaroni and cheese, chicken a la king, gelatin, turkey, mixed vegetables, and even beef stroganoff with noodles.

The cost is only about $2.50 per person per day and even less when purchased in quantity. In addition, each firm packages special items for snacks, survival kits, light lunches which require no cooking and banquets. Your first experience with a freeze-dried steak will delight you.

Care should be taken to measure water accurately for packaged foods. Usually you will need five minutes extra for simmering than is called for on the package. All cooking instructions are printed on the package, so remember not to burn it until the meal is finished!

If you enjoy planning meals on your own, visit the packaged food section of your market. List available main dishes, dried soups, and instant desserts. Bear in mind your cooking limitations. Do not come up with a meal that requires slow baking for two hours! Of course, you can use a reflector oven or dutch oven, but both are time-consuming.

A seven-day menu (see p. 000) is suggested by Duane's Outfitters, Babbitt, Minnesota—an experienced family outfitting service for vacationers in the Boundary Waters Canoe Area. This menu calls for uncooked lunches.

SEVEN-DAY MENU

	1st Day	2d Day	3d Day	4th Day	5th Day	6th Day	7th Day
Breakfast	Bacon and Eggs, Toast, Tang, Coffee or Cocoa	French Toast, Bacon, Syrup, Tang, Coffee or Cocoa	Pancakes, Syrup, Grapefruit Juice, Coffee or Cocoa	Scrambled Eggs, Bacon Bar, Toast, Tang, Coffee, Cocoa	Cooked Cereal, Stewed Fruit, Toast, Coffee or Cocoa	Western Omelet, Toast, Tang, Coffee, Cocoa	French Toast, Syrup, Juice, Coffee, Cocoa
Lunch	Salami Sandwich, Candy Bars, Beverage	American Cheese, Crackers, Jelly, Cookies, Beverage	Summer Sausage Sandwich, Candy Bar, Beverage	Jelly Spread, Bolten Biscuits, Raisins, Cookies, Beverage	Cheddar Cheese Crackers, Mixed Fruit, Beverage	Peanut Butter, Jelly Sandwich, Cookies, Beverage	American Cheese Sandwich, Jelly, Raisins, Candy Bars, Beverage
Dinner	Fresh Beef Patties (groups) or Chicken, Fresh Steaks (individuals) or Chicken. Hash Browns, Peas and Carrots, Gelatin Dessert, Beverage	Ham and Potato Dinner, Green Beans, Pudding, Beverage	Deluxe Beef Stew, Hot Biscuits, Applesauce, Beverage	Beef Stroganoff with Noodles, Peas, Cobbler Dessert, Beverage	Chicken ala King, Hot Biscuits, Corn, Mashed Potatoes, Gelatin Dessert, Beverage	Spaghetti, Mixed Vegetables, Chocolate Pie, Beverage	Beef and Spuds, Carrots, Rice Pudding, Beverage

SOURCE: Duane's Outfitters, Babbitt, Minn.

The foods mentioned above are lightweight with burnable packaging. The weight will run about 20 ounces per person per day. If you have ever carried a week's canned food through the mountains, you will appreciate the difference.

Of course, if cans and bottles are no problem where you are going, and you are prepared to pack out all nonburnable containers, the menu variety is extended more and cooking becomes slightly more simple. If fancy cooking is your hobby, the meals can equal home-cooked fare. With practice you can make drop biscuits, pan breads, doughnuts—almost anything you find time for.

Secure some of the camp cookbooks listed in the bibliography for details on recipes and cooking techniques on the trail. The constant reminder holds here: practice at home under conditions similar to those you will find on the trail!

As you plan each day's menu, write down the needs for each meal. Remember to include such items as seasonings, shortening, condiments and an extra touch for bedtime snacks. Hot chocolate and marshmallows are a favorite. Popcorn is not easily prepared with the usual camp pots, but it can be done. Even cookies and fruit drink will send the children to the tent happy.

Camp Feeding Kinks

It is a good idea to add dried fruits for snacks. Small packages of raisins provide energy during the day. Bowel irregularities are common when the diet changes substantially, and the fruit is useful for good health and dispositions. Remember too that calorie needs for active campers exceed those required at home. Pack candy bars for energy boosters between meals, but avoid chocolate if your trip takes place during hot weather.

Cooking gear has been mentioned elsewhere, but check your menu carefully against the available pots and pans. One of those collapsible plastic water jugs, 2½ or 5 gallon, will spare your largest pot for cooking if you must store water in the camp. Remember cooking utensils and a cleanup kit including scouring pads and dish soap.

Clean dishes provide your best defense against one of the most common camp ailments—upset stomach. Often this results from soiled or unrinsed dishes. Rinse the detergent off thoroughly!

With the growing number of campers, you will want to exercise care with the drinking water even in areas where waters have not been polluted. Purifying pills can be purchased, but you must allow sufficient time for them to work. Any beverage requiring boiling automatically solves the problem. Adding fruit flavoring to drinking water masks the taste of purifying elements which some find unpleasant.

Food storage presents another problem. Most packaged foods need no additional care, but some foods must be kept cool. Toting a cooler through the woods is impractical, except for canoe trips which require few portages. A large burlap or cloth sack will do as well. Place the food to be cooled in watertight plastic, place the plastic bag in the cloth sack and soak it thoroughly. Hang the sack where the breeze can hit it and evaporation will maintain a temperature low enough to preserve even fish fillets all day. This method usually **keeps food** cooler than placing it in the water, unless you are near a cold spring or mountain stream.

The Wilderness Home

Lightweight tents are available at fairly reasonable prices, though good quality in all backpack equipment is essential. The booming camping market has encouraged manufacturers to develop vastly improved products, including featherweight nylon tents.

You will discover the problem with coated, waterproof nylon tents the first morning in camp. Condensation collects on the walls in spite of ventilating windows. Any material that keeps water out will keep it in, too, and the coated nylon fabrics, while wonderfully light, do not breathe as does cotton tent cloth. This is also true of plastic shelters which may appeal because of extremely low prices. Avoid them for serious camping.

While science is solving the condensation problem in moderately-priced backpack tents (it already has in higher-priced styles), many campers continue to use cotton fabrics, installing a waterproof fly over the tent when rain threatens. The variety of fabrics and styles available through camp suppliers will allow you to choose the lightweight tent that suits your needs.

The tent care rules discussed in chapter 3 apply to the trail tent as well. Be sure the ground is fairly level and free of stubble or rocks. You will not be packing a cot! Your foam pad provides insulation and padding, but a hump in the small of your back makes sleep difficult.

A nylon fly is worth its weight for family trips. Should rain fall for long periods, you can keep dry without huddling in the small tent, and you can cook comfortably and keep gear out of the rain.

The question of dangerous animals inevitably arises when wilderness camping is discussed. Anyone who has worked with large domestic animals knows that animals, like humans, come with all kinds of dispositions. You can find maniacs among both men and beasts. The two most commonly feared creatures are snakes and bears.

With normal precautions, you need not fear snakes. If you tease a snake, he may bite. If you surprise a ratler, he will first try to flee, but he will strike if he finds no way to escape. A camp leader reported recently that, unknown to the group at the time, a large rattle snake spent the night in the shelter with several boys without disturbing anyone. The snake apparently appreciated a warm place to sleep!

In some parts of the country you need to guard against toxic insects and poisonous plants, but these are just circumstances of life on the trail. Mosquitos and flies are a worse nuisance than dread bugs, and repellent will handle them.

If you camp in an area inhabited by bears or racoons, you must either construct a rugged "bear box," or hang your food packs out of reach. But hang them high! If you can reach them, so can the bear!

Devising a system to outsmart racoons will tax your ingenuity. They readily open coolers and unsecured food lockers. A suspended pack that will thwart a hungry bear leaves Mr. Racoon undaunted. Use a thin rope or wire which he cannot negotiate. Be on guard against squirrels and mice too. On a hunting trip in Alaska a squirrel car-

ried away every slice of bread we had, leaving us to the
mercy of our sourdough starter and flour sack.

Never leave food in your tent, not even candy treats.
Cosmetics and toothpaste have been known to attract
bears also. A hungry bear will not respect your zippered
tent. He will enter and leave by different routes, leaving
your tent a shambles, and he will carry your food with him.

It is easy to overdramatize the animal dangers in the
woods. The percentage chance of encountering anything
larger than a squirrel is low. There is no evidence to support the idea that either the black bear or the wolf has
ever stalked a man to harm him. Grizzlies and the Alaskan brown bear (a color variant of the grizzly) occasionally seem to attack out of sheer spite, but you will rarely
see one, even when traveling in their home areas.

The natural instinct of all animals is to flee man. If they
feel threatened, and their escape route is blocked, they
may appear to be attacking simply because you are in
their way. Almost all female beasts will attack if they
think their young are in danger. But whatever you read
in books, respect animal life. A frightened, angry black
bear is a formidable creature.

Probably the most dangerous bear is the one that discovers the good taste of campers' food. Bears visit the
garbage dumps regularly and become accustomed to ob-
servers. Some foolish tourist invariably walks too close
to take a picture and the bear reacts, just as a dog reacts
when you try to take his food away from him. Then someone shoots the bear, declaring him to be dangerous.

Male animals tend to become dangerous during mating
season. Bull moose, normally quite docile, will sometimes

rush people or anything that moves, including automobiles. They have been known to charge locomotives on the Alaskan Railroad!

But most encounters wth animals in camp are related to their appetite for your menu, especially when their natural food is not plentiful. You can sleep peacefully if you observe the cautions mentioned above. Never, in hundreds of nights over many years, has my sleep been broken by an animal seeking shelter in my tent.

THE WILDERNESS ETHIC

Family camping is an excellent way to teach children the importance of conservation. Concern for ecology is no mere fad. Human survival depends on mankind making peace with his environment. Surely the Christian should take the lead in exercising good stewardship over the earth.

Building bough beds, erecting pioneer-type bridges and towers, ditching tents, burying garbage; all these belong to the careless past. Those who visit the more remote regions of America or Canada may question this rigid view of man's liberty to mar the earth. But if you travel through some areas as I have which were considered remote just a few years ago, you will understand the wisdom of the wilderness ethic. In one season the age-old beauty can be destroyed.

A view of the camper's relation to the wilderness has been well stated by Gerry Cunningham of the Colorado Outdoors Sports Company of Denver, Colorado:

> Wilderness camping is an experience that is similar in

many respects, but is basically different from Pioneer Camping.

The usual camp program and the majority of camping books still teach the Pioneering Ethic. Skill with the axe, knife, and saw; the construction of some of the comforts of civilization within the wilderness is the gist of most. These programs are variously labeled campcraft, trail-craft, pioneering or survival. Almost all such activities leave their mark on the wilderness: some small irradicable evidence that man has passed this way.

The time has come to realize that we no longer need to pioneer and subdue the wilderness. The time has come to start teaching the *Wilderness Ethic*, which says that man should pass through the wilderness as unobtrusively as the animals do, leaving no sign of his passing. In fact, man's technology has progressed to the point where he can carry a far more comfortable camp on his back than he can build out of the wilderness.

The true wilderness traveler will camp where no one has camped before, and leave no evidence of his tempo-rary use of God's country. Under these conditions, the wilderness will support many many more users than it does at present, and with increased enjoyment by more people will come the guarantee of its preservation.

WILDERNESS TRAVELERS CODE

I will keep my group small. Large herds whether of animals or people leave lasting evidence if they stay too long in one place.

I will not build bough beds or other campcraft projects. There is no need for bough beds with modern sleeping equipment and any display of axemanship to build lean-

tos, picnic table and camp kitchen paraphernalia is entirely out of keeping with appreciation of the wilderness.

I will protect the ground cover. This is one of the most
delicate parts of the wilderness. Such activities as ditching tents, burying garbage and clearing fire circles, destroy in minutes what it may have taken a hundred years
to build up.

I will use small fires. A small Indian fire made of
squaw wood that can be picked up off the ground and
broken in your hands will be much more comfortable to
cook on and will leave a minimum of evidence when you
leave. Instead of clearing a large spot in the forest floor
for a safe fire it is easier to build up such an area on top
of the forest floor with mineral dirt or gravel. The few
rocks used to confine such a fire can be scattered with the
dead charcoal when you leave. This will remove all trace
of your camp.

I will leave no trash. Everything was carried in so if
it cannot be burned it can be carried back out again.
Don't throw it in the bushes and don't bury it. Garbage
and plastic and paper can be burned. Aluminum foil and
cans must be carried out. Some travelers won't have been
as careful of the wilderness as you are, so when you find
their cans and Kleenex "flowers," pick 'em up and pack
'em out.

Trail trips strengthen the spiritual potential inherent
in all family camping. Out there away from traffic and
people, the family shares life with an intimacy not found
elsewhere. A latrine in the bush becomes a magnificent
equalizer. So does the crowded backpack tent. Families
find the sophistications common to urban life quite unnecessary. They can live openly and simply.

This, of course, can be threatening to both parents and children, but until a person allows himself to become vulnerable, the chances for a breakthrough in understanding and acceptance are scant.

When you plan a family trip into the back country, allow time each day for worship. This may prove to be the most authentic worship your family ever experiences, for life on the trail does not lend itself to empty ritual. The spiritual values emerge out of the hearts of people who discover the real presence of Christ within.

9

Camping with Other Families

THE FAMILY CAMPING BOOM has opened a new era in neighborliness. Families are visiting one another again, not at home necessarily, but off in a campground. Once again we must consider the disciplined use of camping to guard against careless neglect of duties at home, but occasionally much benefit can be gained by sharing a camping weekend with other families.

Group family camping takes several forms. A Bible conference or camp may sponsor one or more family weeks each season. We will review the values of this kind of camping. A church or group of churches might conduct a family caravan, with several days devoted to recreation and worship in a public or private campground. And sometimes an informal group of camping friends from one church share a few days together at a nearby park.

FAMILY WEEK AT CAMP

After several years of struggle, resident camps seem to have discovered the secret for successful family programs. The secret can be summed up in one phrase: *meeting real needs.* Early failures resulted from misunderstanding the family's wishes. A typical program often was little more than a modification of the regular youth camp program;

109

a string of meetings and classes graded in Sunday school fashion. The family spent little time together other than for meals and sleeping. A few camps even attempted to house men and boys in one set of cabins and women and girls in another.

Then creative minds went to work. Cabins were modified to accommodate two families, and where this proved unfeasible, registration was limited to the number of single family housing units the camp could provide. The program was overhauled to provide maximum time for family activity, yet with some periods for adults while the children enjoyed supervised activity. The relaxed schedule included many options to meet varied family interests.

Family program ideas are still evolving, but climbing registrations indicate that successful principles have been discovered. Family camp represents one of the few church-related programs serving the family as a unit. Hopefully, some of the concepts will be carried back home for use the rest of the year.

Effective programming blends graded periods with a strong emphasis on all-family activity. The regular camp staff leads young people and children while parents meet for morning Bible study and discussion. Nursery and baby sitting service may be provided, freeing every family member to participate. An hour or more prior to lunch the family gets together for a swim, a visit to the craft shop, or some other activity of general interest.

The afternoon may include a rest period for the children, a time even adults appreciate! Then there is time for recreation, field trips or family competition in arts and crafts, with every family member participating. The en-

tire camp facility allows parents and children to play together. Dads are sternly warned against sneaking off for
golf, leaving the kids with Mom. Of course, an all-family
golf tournament might be planned.

Families eat together, perhaps two families at a table,
with a plan to rotate families each day. Frequently breakfast is served over an extended period to accommodate
different rising habits. Family-style meals replace the buf-
fet line commonly found in youth camps. This kind of
camping gives Mom a real vacation.

The evening includes an all-family gathering with skits,
pantomime (guess Dad's occupation), fun songs and
awards (trophy for the best family-built sand castle or
table centerpiece). A gifted speaker may address the entire camp, or a missionary may minister, guiding families
in worship as a group, with a blend of devotional and
evangelistic moods.

At the close of the day families may move to the fire
circle for vespers, or perhaps the families could launch out
in boats for a Galilean service. Evening programs always
focus on the family, with vitality and variety to build interest, then the younger children are brought to the cabins
and tucked into bed.

They learn that a security patrol remains within earshot
constantly. Mom and Dad are free to slip away for adult
fellowship and refreshments, while teenagers enjoy a program under staff supervision in another part of the camp.

Each morning and evening parents spend time together
sharing the burdens and blessings of raising a family. They
talk and pray, and perhaps take a moonlight cruise. Peace
and joy spread their benediction over the camp as parents

share and make new friends. Little wonder that family camp is the fastest-growing dimension of Christian camping in the seventies.

FAMILY CARAVAN CAMPING

The family caravan comes closer to the purpose of this book since each family arrives hauling its own housing. Many Bible camps and conferences are expanding tent and trailer facilities to accommodate the growing demand, creating the possibility for enlarging family activity at the camp. Usually, however, the caravan gathers at a private or public camping area for a long weekend.

A while ago I participated in a most stimulating family caravan which I reported in the May, '72 *Moody Monthly*. A condensation of this article will portray the great potential in this kind of camping for your family.

*   *   *

"Ready or not, here I come."

This, in the once-familiar language of childhood, seems to sum up what family camping is saying to the church today. And churches are trying camping programs, for Christian families are going camping in numbers unequaled since the passing of the frontier camp meeting.

In 1971 I shared in a Memorial Day weekend program that persuaded me that family camping can be a blessing both to the church and the home. Taking advantage of the long weekend, the Great Plains Baptist Conference invited families to converge at an out-of-the-way public campsite.

Thirty-seven families came, totally some one hundred

sixty people of all ages—with tents, motor homes, pick up campers and trailers.

The genius of the project was minimal program. Families made up their own programs. They made the most of outdoor living, freedom from schedules and opportunities to visit. The result was a unanimous request to repeat the caravan.

Church families have been caught up in the national camping trend. Why? One reason is time. The extended weekend is here to stay; many believe the four-day week is just around the corner.

A number of communities are experimenting with revised school schedules, breaking the traditional summer vacations into several relatively brief vacation periods. Work vacations are longer and retirement for many is beginning at an earlier age.

Families have more money, too. With more time and money, families have many options, but camping continues to be a favorite vacation for increasing numbers, church families included.

Along with changing calendars and economics is a change in mood. The disenchantment with mere materialism and secularism has spread beyond youth. What was once considered a passing back-to-nature fad is now being seen as a reflection of real need.

Ecological concern, the deliberate move toward simpler life styles and the renewed interest in spiritual things suggest that many are looking for something better than freeways and stock markets. All this adds up to unprecedented opportunity for the church to serve its people and reach out to the lost world through family camping.

Nonprogramming is the key to this kind of family camping. Do not overplan! There is something about rigid schedules and a multiplicity of activity that destroys the spontaneity essential to natural family life. There must be planning to be sure, and Bible studies or campfires may well be offered. But the focus should remain on the family unit with as little interference as possible.

What about competing with the church's regular Sunday services? Ultimately the local church will have to weigh the spiritual values of a Christian family camping experience against the effects of absences. Church duties should be covered; arrangements for substitutes in Sunday school, pulpit and other leadership roles should be definite and complete. In my thinking it is perfectly legitimate to count the people who gather at camp as church attenders if statistics are a burden.

Certainly it should be recognized that the church is people, not the building. Some of the church may gather in the building, some by a campfire; both groups are the church with equal potential for worshiping and meeting with God. In fact, one of the great values of family camping is linked with the discovery by Christians that true worship does not depend on a day, an hour or a place. Wherever God's people gather, the church is present.

This is the philosophy of effective family camping for church groups. Let's turn now to the steps involved in arranging and leading a family camping caravan for a church or group of churches.

1. *Select a date and place.* The long weekend is ideal, but bear in mind that the rest of America will be camping during the same period. Finding a place where several

families can camp together may pose a problem. Any weekend with generally favorable weather in prospect can be acceptable.

The place should not be too difficult to find. Published camping guides list thousands of small, private campgrounds scattered throughout the countryside which are happy to accommodate groups of family campers. Facilities may be relatively primitive or fully modern. Often there will be a beach on the site or nearby, fishing ponds, and trails for hiking and riding.

Public campgrounds may accommodate, though overcrowding is already a problem and reservations usually are not possible. While the church out camping never seeks to shun people, finding a place with enough camp sites may rule out the public facilities for group camping.

A growing number of Christian camps and conferences are developing family camping centers with modern hookups for trailers and other facilities normally found in public and private camping areas. Churches have been known to arrange with a sympathetic farmer to camp on his property. In off-seasons, private campgrounds near heavily traveled routes welcome group reservations, making their recreation and service facilities available at reasonable rates.

Thought should be given to the kinds of activity available within reasonable distance of the camp site. The area used in the Great Plains caravan last Memorial Day took advantage of a guest ranch adjacent to the camp. Horses, wagon rides, a burro and a small museum provided interesting activities for families. The river offered fishing and open country provided miles of hiking trails.

Costs for family camping are modest. Since each family provides its own food and lodging, a small registration fee will cover promotional and operation expenses. Each family will pay for space rental, usually not more than $5 per day. Public camps may cost nothing.

2. *Plan a devotional program.* I have already warned against over-programming. Many families need to be encouraged to plan activity together. In my opinion the whole purpose of family camping is destroyed if a highly-developed schedule fragments the family through the day. I favor two all-camp gatherings each day with participation on a voluntary basis. This places the burden on program planners to attract a response.

Plan a morning Bible hour aimed at the entire family. This may be a simple presentation from Scripture with singing, sharing and prayer for the day. That is enough. And please, no extended sermonizing! Let the delight of the occasion be the message; the love one for another, the sheer fact of life in Christ Jesus. A brief time together in the morning after breakfast will set the tone for the day.

Let prayer meetings be spontaneous. Encourage family prayers. Perhaps a simple Scripture outline can be passed out for families who need help. Keep the emphasis on individual families getting together for devotions. Let small-group Bible studies be spontaneous too—two or three families meeting together, creating their own schedule and leadership.

The evening campfire can be offered at sunset; this is a time for song and sharing once again. A brief devotional thought and perhaps vocal or instrumental music suitable to the setting will enrich the time.

Why at sunset? To reserve the darkness for family campfires. I enjoy the memory of standing at dusk following sunset vespers and watching twenty or more small fires spring up to form a huge circle in the gathering spring darkness. Each fire marked a family, or two families meeting together. I heard laughter, shouts, a snatch of song; a guitar strummed to a youthful beat; instead of one huge campfire with one voice speaking, there were a score of campfires and scores of voices sharing the joy of being God's child. This was true family camping.

At our camp last spring each family set its own schedule and planned and cooked its own meals, save for one grand breakfast where I served sourdough flapjacks for everyone. Each family found its own recreation, though many spontaneous ball games and horseshoe matches developed during the camp period.

At your church camp, you might see that someone brings a volleyball and net, horseshoes, a ball and bat and those marvelous plastic discs called frisbies. But avoid highly organized tournaments. Let families play together. You can be sure someone will produce a football.

Investigate the recreation opportunities in the general area and pass the word around. A riding stable with gentle horses always appeals to young people. Under certain conditions you may wish to organize a hike or a group tour for those who wish to participate, but focus on the family being together. Never program apartness; the natural inclinations of children, youth and adults will create groupings at appropriate times through the day on their own.

3. *Practice Cautions.* Avoid a demanding travel route. Try to keep driving distances as low as possible without

sacrificing interest. Few people would respond to family camping on the edge of their own town. Begin and conclude the program at convenient hours which will not demand hurried driving.

Restrict participation to families. A group of unattached young people without parental supervision can prove disruptive. A family may bring a guest, but youth group camping and family camping are not always compatible. Should unsupervised young people show up, assign some responsible man to manage the situation. It may not be possible to require that they leave, but they should not be permitted to interfere with the family purpose.

Check the camping area for safety hazards, especially rivers or lakes. Warn parents of dangers, and remind them that they are responsible for their children. Check for toxic plants and provide cautions. Investigate camping and fire regulations, firewood sources; check on the availability of safe water and adequacy of toilet facilities.

Expect practices that may not be acceptable among Christians if you camp among others. Drinking, smoking and offensive language are normal parts of life in the world, but indulgence in them by others need not interfere with the enjoyment of your group. A friendly, open spirit to neighbors will be appreciated, with the sunset campfire a natural medium for sharing Christ. Invite everyone.

Be sure your witness is supported by good camping manners! Obey the rules; leave a clean camp; show helpfulness and courtesy to everyone. You may find a service project every family can share to improve the camping area and show that Christians are concerned for the beauty and preservation of our world.

A final caution. Do not overdo group family camping! One good experience a year is better than repeated outings which may create problems of programming and tensions in the Sunday school staff. The congregation and its orderly program of training and outreach deserve careful respect. Worship may take place anywhere in any size group, but the discipline of public worship seems essential for Christian growth. Camping must not become a sort of spiritual anarchy, but a means of renewal and benediction for God's people.*

FELLOWSHIP CAMPING

The third variety of group camping finds several families from a church, planning a trip together. Usually they will base in one park rather than moving day by day. No formal program is required. The days are spent in friendly, spontaneous fun, with many unstructured discussions of mutual concerns.

One church of my acquaintance spends several weekends each summer this way, with the pastor and various families sharing at different times. An informal evening campfire attracts neighboring campers, who are invited to stop by for outdoor worship Sunday morning. Some believe that church families touch more unchurched homes with a witness for Christ through these family fellowship camps than the church reaches through regular channels all year!

Family camping opens the door to the benefits of old-fashioned friendship that seemed to slip away from us

*Lloyd D. Mattson, "A Family Camp for Your Church," *Moody Monthly*, May 1972, pp. 38-39, 103-7. Used by permission.

somewhere. Perhaps we hunger for a better way of life. Whatever the causes, millions of families have taken up the camping habit, and much good can result.

10

Camping Carry-overs

IN THIS CLOSING CHAPTER I would like to call your attention to an important cause. The world is full of causes, as your mail will attest. But this cause demands your attention, because without your help it is a *lost cause*. You may have to give up other causes, some important ones. You might lose money in missed sales or lost overtime at the plant. Some of your friends might even become offended, but that is the price of a cause.

The cause, of course, is your home, the people who make up your family, the most important institution on the face of the earth.

HELPING THE FAMILY GROW

Throughout these pages I have tried to promote camping as a way to help your family grow. But camping is only one way, and a limited way at that. Family life should be an entity, not a collection of parts. It is difficult to have a happy camping life and a miserable church life. The opposite is also true. Family happiness results from a total experience. For your children, the joy of the Lord begins with fun in the family whatever form that fun may take.

This all goes back to that dreadful dichotomy, the spiritual versus the secular. Christian parents and children must learn that Jesus is always and equally present no matter what day or hour, and no matter what place or activity.

If you are to serve your personal cause, you must recognize the *real* needs of family members; children need your *time*. I say this, because having read this book, many will agree that they should spend more time with their family, and they will—some day. But with a family there is no *some day*.

What has happened in your home recently that the children remember with delight? And equally important, what are they looking forward to with eagerness? It may not be camping, but something worthwhile from the child's perspective should be on the horizon.

The trip you plan for your next vacation can fill the whole year with pleasure. Mark the maps, unfold the travel folders and brochures describing the area you plan to visit, and check out interesting side trips. Let the whole family share in planning. This extends the joy of camping through weeks and months.

Of course you will show the slides from last year's trip now and then. If you have never discovered photography, do so at once! You will find the cost is modest, and the new cameras almost foolproof. Let every member of the family try his hand at it. A child loves to say, "I took *that* picture!" Last summer's camping trip can last a long, long time.

THE CHURCH ON THE CORNER

Blessed is the church that allows families to share their

joys. How pleasant those Sunday evenings when our congregation meets in the fellowship hall following the service for refreshments and sharing. Each family is allowed to show a dozen slides, or one family may be featured to tell of their unusual vacation. When the presentation includes reports of a fellowship camp that many families shared, the evening becomes richer yet.

My itinerant life these past years has carried me to hundreds of churches throughout the U.S. and Canada, usually as a guest preacher. I have come to sense the vitality of a church by the way people relate to each other. Many churches conduct aesthetically superior programs, with dignified music of professional quality. The people enter, sit quietly, and leave. In other churches neither the music nor the program can compare, but the people seem alive! They smile at one another and chat pleasantly, which some claim disturbs the preservice spirit of worship. But I am not sure that it does.

I love to stand at the close of the service and watch the people blend into companies of friendship, each according to his age and personality. I hear the good words that described another company of Christians, "Behold, how they love one another."

What I like most is to see children enjoying themselves, even though they sometimes forget churchly decorum. The saddest scene I can imagine is the youngster, often a young teenager, sitting in a pew, sullen and alone, waiting for his parents to finish talking so he can go on to pleasant things. That boy could be one of yours or mine, and he is the cause I plead.

A Young Man's Burden

We have found camping a source of strength for our family. I think you will too. The skills your children learn and the attitudes they form while camping can shape their lives. Man can no longer be permitted to exploit the earth for his short-term gain. Who thought about conserving air or water a generation ago? It was taken for granted that they would always be there. We know now that man can destroy even the oceans. Conservation and Christian stewardship are parts of the same issue, for to waste natural resources is to steal from tomorrow's children.

It seemed a small thing when my children were young to break away from pastoral duties for an outing. Those times were too few. Big problems pressed in; at least they seemed big then. I have forgotten now what they were. I thought that little children would always be around, to be served when there was time. I know now that that is not true.

You will lose your children before you know it; and if you are careless, you may lose them long before they leave home. We never know what moment of time plants the seed of faith and understanding that can change a child's whole life. I found that out not long ago.

There is a letter in my file written from Indiana University by a lonely freshman. It is one of those letters a father waits for, the kind that brings past years close to home. My son, Dave, wrote the letter.

He wrote to say thanks to his mother and me, to say "I love you," and to unburden his heart. He told us how he had come as close as a boy can come to marking his life by tragedy. He had been spared because he remembered what I had taught him.

The letter recounted a fishing trip in Alaska. I remember the trip well, for I took my largest trout that day. A 31-inch steelhead! Not a record breaker, but a satisfying fish. I lost several huge king salmon. They were just too much fish for my tackle. My memories involved fishing, but Dave remembered something else.

Shooting and hunting have not been a big thing in my life, though I enjoy a hunting camp with a bunch of men. But I am not impressed by beef-eating critics who carp at the careful sportsman who enjoys the challenge of hunting! We have enjoyed plinking with a .22 rifle, and I took care to impress on my children the constant danger of all firearms.

Three rules governed the use of guns in our home: (1) Always assume a gun is loaded even when you are sure it is not; (2) Never point a gun at anything you do not intend to shoot; (3) Never pull the trigger until you are absolutely sure of your target.

We had added a single-shot .22 rifle to our fishing gear as we left Anchorage for Deep Creek on the Kenai Peninsula that early summer morning. Dave was perhaps ten years old. The weather was gray, with mist falling now and then. After a brief search, we located a spot for our small tent and set up camp not far from the stream.

The high water and brushy banks soon discouraged Dave's fishing, and he sought other diversions. A trail led between the stream and a low gravel bank, a safe situation for plinking. The ubiquitous beer cans provided imaginary varmints, and I would be nearby, fishing a stretch of Deep Creek. I gave Dave permission to shoot.

The mist had turned to a light rain now, and I felt my cotton cap getting wet. Half in jest and half seriously, I fashioned a protective beanie from aluminum foil and slapped it over the crown of my cap. A handsome rig it was! I set off upstream to fish and Dave took out after imaginary lions and bears.

All of that I remembered without Dave's letter; the rest he told me. A fisherman's patience outlasts a lion hunter's anytime, and Dave began to search about for more challenging targets. He knew the rules. Always shoot against a safe background. Across the stream he saw another gravel bank through the brush. Now for a target.

A shiny, crumpled tin can caught his eye a respectable distance away, partly hidden by the brush. Slowly he raised his rifle, taking careful aim. Then the cautions I had hammered home pressed in: *every gun is loaded, never aim at what you do not expect to shoot,* and *never pull the trigger until you are sure, dead sure.* An instant before firing, he lowered the rifle to check the target. He saw it move.

Dave had my head, encased in the foolish aluminum beanie, centered in his sights! He had not seen me through the bushes wading in the stream. All he saw was the silver glint of my hat; and if he had fired, he probably would not have missed.

That is quite a burden for a boy to carry through a decade. Had Dave pulled the trigger and the bullet found its mark, I probably would never have known it. The loss would not have been mine, for I met the Saviour many years ago. But my son would have spent his life remembering a moment of carelessness, and that would have been my fault, not his. I put the gun in his hands.

We parents place in our children's hands and hearts the potential for great good or great harm. We invest in them physical and spiritual energies that can destroy them in a moment, and others with them. We do not always prepare them as well as we should to cope with those life forces.

I am glad I taught my son to shoot, for his sake and mine. I have never regretted the time I spent with him, though I wish it could have been more. I pray that the days I gave to my children might help them face the inevitable crises of life and perhaps, now and then, some word from Mom and Dad might echo in their hearts and spare them sorrow.

Our children are grown now, and I am thankful to say that they are more than a daughter and four sons. We count them as five of our choicest friends. We enjoy talking with them, and sometimes we marvel at their discernment. They are people who must find their own place in God's pattern, and I wish them well. That is all I can do for them now. Someday perhaps we will have them all home again. It has been a long time.

But in a sense they are still around. That box of snap shots we are going to sort and mount someday hold them here. And those slides! Elsie and I smile as we screen them—that first long camping trip to Alaska; Joel's first salmon from Bird Creek; barefoot Kevin, now with moustache and sideburns, playing a Christmas ukulele at three; Sally, a lovely girl, marching with the band; Keith, our oldest son, now the pastor of two small churches; and Dave, the athlete and first-class gymnast, who wrote to say, "Thanks. I love you."

If you want good memories, you have to work at it, and you have very little time. Camping played a big part in our family life. I hope you will find it rewarding too.

Sources of Information and Equipment

FAMILY CAMPING CLUBS

THE BOOM in family camping has given rise to many national, regional, and local camping clubs. Others are certain to appear. You will find help by sharing experiences through membership in one or more of these associations. Denominational and interdenominational Christian camping fellowships for families are appearing, adding a further enrichment to the travel club idea. Most fellowships publish magazines or newsletters.

Campers on Mission; Special Mission Ministries, Home Mission Board; 1350 Spring Street, N.W.; Atlanta, Ga. 30309

Christian Camping International, Box 400, Somonauk, Ill. 60552

Christian Family Camping Association, Box 562, Pontiac, Mich. 48056

Lutheran Family Campers Association, Box 84, Narberth, Pa. 19072

Camping Club of America, 996 National Press Building, Washington, D.C. 20004

National Campers and Hikers Association, 7172 Transit Road, Buffalo, N.Y. 14221

North American Family Campers Association, Box 308, Newbury, Mass. 01950

CHRISTIAN FAMILY CAMPING PROGRAMS

For those who desire family camping adventures with other Christians, a variety of programs are being developed by Christian camps. Camping caravans, camper rallies, resident family weeks, and wilderness trips are opportunities which will prove especially helpful to the beginning camper. For a family camping bulletin, write *Christian Camping International*, Box 400, Somonauk, Illinois 60056.

BOOKS FOR THE CAMPING FAMILY

Reading can enrich the camping experience for every family member. Here is a representative list of books on camping and the outdoors that will prove helpful in preparing for family camping. Asterisks mark titles of special value. The list could be greatly extended, and new titles appear regularly. Prices are subject to change.

Angier, Bradford. *Home in Your Pack*. Harrisburg, Pa.: Stackpole, 1965.
———. *Skills for Taming the Wilds*. Harrisburg, Pa.: Stackpole, n.d.
———. *Wilderness Cookery*. Harrisburg, Pa.: Stackpole, 1960.
Bates, Joseph D., Jr. *The Outdoor Cook's Bible*. New York: Doubleday, 1964. $1.95, paper.
Boy Scouts of America. *Fieldbook for Boys and Men*. New York: McGraw-Hill, 1967. 565 pp. $1.95, paper.
Chappell, Wallace. *When You Go Trail Camping*. Martinsville, Ind.: American Camping Assoc., 1969.
Germain, Donald L. *When You Go Canoe Camping*. Martinsville, Ind.: American Camping Assoc., 1968. Order from ACA, Bradford Woods, Martinsville, Ind. 46151. 69 pp. 75¢, paper.

Golden Nature Guide Series. New York: Golden Press. For general background on the outdoors, this series is unexcelled. The titles include *Amphibians, Trees, Insects, Stars, Reptiles, Birds, Flowers, Mammals, Fishes, Seashore, Weather, Rocks and Minerals, The American Southwest, The American Southeast, The American Northwest*.

*Hammett, Catherine T. *Your Own Book of Campcraft*. New York: Simon and Schuster, Pocket Books, 1971. 197 pp. 95¢, paper.

Hamper, Stan. *Wilderness Survival*. 1963. Order from author, 405 W. High St., Dowagiac, Mich. 97 pp. $1.00.

Jaeger, Ellsworth. *Wildwood Wisdom*. New York: Macmillan, 1966.

Janes, Edward C. *Nelson's Encyclopedia of Camping*. Appleton, Wis.: Nelson, 1963.

Johnson, James R. *Anyone Can Camp in Comfort*. New York: McKay, 1964.

Knobel, Bruno. *Camping Out*. New York: Sterling, 1962.

Lynn, Gordon. *Golden Book of Camping*. Rev. ed. New York: Golden, 1971. 112 pp. $3.95.

Mattson, Lloyd D. *Camping With Families*. Wheaton, Ill.: Scripture Press, 1973. Outlines patterns for planning group family camping. 32 pp. 39¢.

———. *The Wilderness Way*. Christian Camping International, 1970. 60 pp. $1.00.

McKay, Joy. *Raindrops Keep Falling on My Tent*. Wheaton, Ill.: Scripture Press, 1973. Offers delightful suggestions for rainy day activities with children. 32 pp. 39¢.

*Merrill, W. K. *All About Camping*. Harrisburg, Pa.: Stackpole, 1970. 399 pp. $2.95, paper.

*Miracle, Leonard, and Decker, Maurice H. *The Complete Book of Camping*. New York: Harper, 1962.

*Newman, James, and Newman, Barbara. *The Family Camping Guide*. New York: World, 1966. 244 pp. Paper.

Ormond, Clyde. *Complete Book of Outdoor Lore.* New York: Harper, 1964.

*Riviere, Bill. *The Camper's Bible.* New York: Doubleday, 1970. 176 pp. $1.95, paper.

———. *Family Campers' Cookbook.* New York: Holt, Rinehart, & Winston, 1965.

*Rutstrum, Calvin. *The New Way of the Wilderness.* New York: Macmillan, 1966.

Shuttlesworth, Dorothy E. *Exploring Nature With Your Child.* Minneapolis: Denison, 1952.

Stephens, Mae Webb, and Wells, George S. *Coping with Camp Cooking.* Harrisburg, Pa.: Stackpole, 1966.

Sunset Camping Handbook. 3d ed. Menlo Park, Calif.: Lane, 1962.

Wells, George, and Wells, Iris. *Handbook of Wilderness Travel.* New York: Harper, 1956.

*Wells, George S. *Modern ABC's of Family Camping.* Harrisburg, Pa.: Stackpole, 1967.

Whelen, Townsend, and Angier, Bradford. *On Your Own in the Wilderness.* Harrisburg, Pa.: Stackpole, 1958.

Zuck, Roy, and Getz, Gene, eds. *Ventures in Family Living.* Chicago: Moody, 1971. $1.95, paper. An excellent resource for building family life.

CAMPING MAGAZINES

Up-to-date information on places to go and products to make camping enjoyable can be secured from outdoor magazines. Here are several of special value to the family camper.

Better Camping, 500 Hyacinth Place, Highland Park, Ill. 60035
The Campfire Chatter, P.O. Box 308, Newburyport, Mass. 01950
Camping and Trailering Guide, P.O. Box 1014, Grass Valley, Calif. 95945

Journal of Christian Camping, Box 400, Somonauk, Ill. 60056
Trails Away, 109 N. LaFayette St., Greenville, Mich. 48838

NATIONAL, STATE, AND PROVINCIAL CAMPING INFORMATION SOURCES

A letter addressed to these offices will bring you details about camping opportunities in state parks, along with official tourist information bulletins. Provincial offices will supply information concerning Canada's unequalled camping areas. Additional help can be secured by writing or phoning the Canadian Tourist Bureau in your nearest large city.

NATIONAL

Federal Reservoirs: U.S. Corps of Engineers, Dept. of the Army, Washington, D.C. 20315

Indian Reservations: Bureau of Indian Affairs, U.S. Dept. of the Interior, Washington, D.C. 20240

National Forests: Forest Service, U.S. Dept. of Agriculture, Washington, D.C. 20240

National Parks: National Park Service, U.S. Dept. of the Interior, Washington, D.C. 20240

Wildlife Refuges: Fish and Wildlife Service, U.S. Dept. of the Interior, Washington, D.C. 20240

INDIVIDUAL STATES

Alabama: Department of Conservation, State Capitol, Montgomery, Ala. 36104

Alaska: Alaska Travel Division, Box 2391, Juneau, Alaska 99801

Arizona: Arizona Development Board, 1500 W. Jefferson St., Phoenix, Ariz. 85007

Arkansas: Publicity and Parks Commission, State Capitol, Little Rock, Ark. 72201

California: Division of Beaches and Parks, P.O. Box 2390, Sacramento, Calif. 95811

Colorado: Department of Public Relations, State Capitol, Denver, Colo. 80203

Connecticut: Parks and Forest Commission, State of Connecticut, Hartford, Conn. 06115

Delaware: State Park Commission, 3300 Faulkland Road, Wilmington, Del. 19808

District of Columbia: National Capital Region, National Park Service, 1100 Ohio Dr., S.W., Washington, D.C. 20242

Florida: Florida Park Service, 101 W. Gaines St., Tallahassee, Fla. 32301

Georgia: Department of State Parks, 7 Hunter St., S.W., Atlanta, Ga. 30334

Hawaii: Division of State Parks, State of Hawaii, P.O. Box 621, Honolulu, Hawaii 96809

Idaho: Department of Commerce and Development, State House, Boise, Idaho

Illinois: Illinois Division of Parks and Memorials, 100 State Office Bldg., Springfield, Ill. 62706

Indiana: Division of State Parks, 16 State Office Bldg., Indianapolis, Ind. 46209

Iowa: State Conservation Commission, East 7th and Court Ave., Des Moines, Iowa 50309

Kansas: State Park and Resources Authority, 801 Harrison, Topeka, Kan. 66612

Kentucky: Travel Division, Dept. of Public Information, Capitol Annex Bldg., Frankfort, Ky. 40601

Louisiana: State Parks and Recreation Commission, Old State Capitol Bldg., Baton Rouge, La. 70821

Maine: State Park and Recreation Commission, State House Office Bldg., Augusta, Me. 04330

Maryland: Department of Forests and Parks, State Office Bldg., Annapolis, Md. 21404

Massachusetts: Division of Parks and Forests, 15 Ashburton Pl., Boston, Mass. 02108

Michigan: Michigan Tourist Council, Stevens T. Mason Bldg., Lansing, Mich. 48926

Minnesota: Division of State Parks, 320 Centennial Office Bldg., St. Paul, Minn. 55101

Mississippi: State Park System, 1102 Woolfolk Bldg., Jackson, Miss. 39201

Missouri: State Park Board, 1206 Jefferson Bldg., Jefferson City, Mo. 65102

Montana: Montana Highway Commission, Helena, Mont. 59601

Nebraska: Nebraska Game, Forestation and Parks Commission, State Capitol, Lincoln, Neb. 68509

Nevada: State Park System, Carson City, Nev. 89701

New Hampshire: Division of Economic Development, State House Annex, Concord, N.H. 03301

New Jersey: Dept. of Conservation and Economic Development, P.O. Box 1889, Trenton, N.J. 08625

New Mexico: State Tourist Div., 302 Galisteo, Santa Fe, N.M. 87501

New York: Division of State Parks, State Campus Site, Albany, N.Y. 12226

North Carolina: Travel Information Div., Dept. of Conservation & Development, Raleigh, N.C. 27602

North Dakota: North Dakota Travel Dept., State Capitol, Bismarck, N.D. 58501

Ohio: Division of Parks and Recreation, 1500 Dublin Rd., Columbus, Ohio 43212

Oklahoma: Div. of State Parks, Rm. 533, State Capitol Bldg., Oklahoma City, Okla. 73105

Oregon: State Highway Dept., Salem, Ore. 97310

Pennsylvania: State Dept. of Forests and Waters, Harrisburg, Pa. 17120

Rhode Island: Rhode Island Development Council, Roger Williams Bldg., Hayes St., Providence, R.I. 02908

South Carolina: South Carolina Development Bd., Columbia, S.C. 29202

South Dakota: Dept. of Game, Fish and Parks, Pierre, S.D. 57501

Tennessee: Division of State Parks, 235 Cordell Hull Bldg., Nashville, Tenn. 37219

Texas: Texas State Parks Board, Drawer E, Capitol Station, Austin, Tex. 78701

Utah: Tourist and Publicity Council, State Capitol, Salt Lake City, Utah 84114

Vermont: Department of Forests and Parks, Montpelier, Vt. 05601

Virginia: Division of Public Relations and Advertising, 811 State Office Bldg., Richmond, Va. 23219

Washington: Parks and Recreation Commission, 522 S. Franklin, Olympia, Wash. 98502

West Virginia: Division of Parks and Recreation, State Office Bldg., Charleston, W. Va. 25305

Wisconsin: Vacation and Travel Service, Box 450, Madison, Wis. 53701

Wyoming: Travel Commission, 2320 Capitol Ave., Cheyenne, Wyo. 82001

PROVINCIAL

Alberta: Government Travel Bureau, 331 Highways Bldg., Edmonton, Alta.

British Columbia: Government Travel Bureau, Parliament Bldg., Victoria, B.C.

Manitoba: Bureau of Travel and Publicity, Legislative Bldg., Winnipeg, Man.

New Brunswick: Travel Bureau, 196 Queen St., Fredericton, N.B.

Newfoundland: Tourist Development Office, St. John's, Nfld
Nova Scotia: Nova Scotia Travel Bureau, Halifax, N.S.
Ontario: Dept. of Tourism, 67 College St., Toronto, Ont.
Prince Edward Island: Travel Bureau, P.O. Box 1087, Charlottetown, P.E.I.
Quebec: Dept. of Tourism, 12 Ste. Anne St., Quebec, P.Q.
Saskatchewan: Tourist Development Branch, Power Bldg., Regina, Sask.
Yukon Territory: Department of Travel and Publicity, Whitehorse, Y.T.

OTHER SOURCES

The more you learn and prepare in advance, the greater will be your family enjoyment. A wealth of material awaits you from tourist bureaus and local chamber of commerce offices. Here are samples of information sources you will find helpful for trip planning.

CAMPING AND VACATION SHOWS

Most metropolitan areas host a vacation travel exposition with exhibits from vacation areas, resorts, camping equipment suppliers, outfitters, and other vacation-related enterprises. Many family camping opportunities can be discovered here.

CAMPGROUND GUIDES

Several directories of private and public campgrounds are published, listing the location and facilities for each · campground. These directories are invaluable for planning the travel itinerary. Frequently you can phone reservations ahead to assure a camping spot. Prices listed are subject to change.

Border-to-Border Camping Trips, by Glenn and Dale Rhodes (\$2.95). Stackpole Co., Cameron and Kelker Streets, Harrisburg, Pa. 17105

Campground Guide for Tent and Trailers, by Robert O. Klotz, Sr., (\$1.50). Campgrounds Unlimited, Blue Rapids, Kans. 66411

Camping Maps, Canada, by Glenn and Dale Rhodes (\$1.95). Box 862, Upper Mountclair, N.J. 07042

Handbook of Auto Camping and Motorist's Guide to Public Campgrounds, by George and Iris Wells (\$4.95). Harper and Row, 49 E. 33d St., New York, N.Y. 10016

Rand McNally Guidebook to Campgrounds (\$3.95, paper); *Rand McNally Road Atlas* (Annual. \$2.75, paper); *Rand McNally Travel Trailer Guide* (Annual. \$3.95). Rand McNally & Co., P.O. Box 7600, Chicago, Ill. 60680

Woodall's Trailering Parks and Campgrounds Directory (Annual. \$3.95, paper). Woodall Publishing Co., 500 Hyacinth Place, Highland Park, Ill. 60035

NATIONAL PARK AND FOREST INFORMATION

More than 300 million acres of public lands await family campers in the US and Canada, including some of the most magnificent wilderness areas of the world. Whether you plan a trail trip or an auto travel trek, you will want to enjoy the national and provincial camping areas.

A wide variety of publications related to camping can be obtained from:

Superintendent of Documents
US Government Printing Office
Washington, D.C. 20402

You may write for a free listing of available publications.

Be sure to specify your interests, such as the area you would like to visit and the type of camping or outdoor sport you are interested in.

The following publications are recommended and can be ordered from the Superintendent of Documents:

Backpacking in the National Forest Wilderness: A Family Adventure. 15¢

Camping in the National Park System. A guide to fees, facilities, etc. 25¢

Camping: Outdoors Calling You? A Forest Service booklet. 20¢

National Forest Vacations. A Forest Service booklet. 45¢

National Forest Wilderness and Primitive Areas. Map of 88 wilderness areas in 14 states. 15¢

National Park System Maps

National Parks, Historical Sites, and National Monuments.

National Wildlife Refuges. 35¢

Reclamation's Recreational Opportunities. 25¢

Room to Roam. A recreation guide to the public lands of the West. 75¢

Wilderness

Trail Food Distributors

Here are some firms that manufacture packaged foods for trail camping. You will find their literature helpful and their services a great saving of time. Sporting goods stores and camping centers frequently stock their merchandise.

Bernard Food Industries, Inc.; 217 N. Jefferson St.; Chicago, Ill. 60606

Chuck Wagon Foods, 176 Oak St., Newton, Mass. 02164

Dri-Lite Foods, 8716 Santa Fe Ave., South Gate, Calif. 90280

C. F. Emiling Co., 2305 W. Erie St., Chicago, Ill. 60612

S. Gumpert Co., Inc.; 812 Jersey Ave.; Jersey City, N.J. 07302
 (Trip-Lites)

Hilker and Bletsch, 2200 Lunt Ave., Elk Grove Village, Ill.
 60007 (Tripperoos)

J. B. Kisky Co., 1829 N.E. Alberta St., Portland, Oreg. 97211
 (Trail Meals)

Ad. Seidel and Son, Inc.; 2323 Pratt Blvd.; Elk Grove Village,
 Ill. 60007

Stow-a-Way Products Co., Inc.; 103 Ripley Rd.; Cohasset,
 Mass. 02025

Wyler & Co., 2500 W. Addison St., Chicago, Ill. 60618

CAMPING EQUIPMENT

Camping supply centers can be found in most major
shopping areas. You will find it helpful and educational to
browse through the catalogs from the firms listed below to
acquaint your family with the array of equipment available for your camping comfort. You can plan your budget
as well, and discover the price ranges for essential gear.

Abercrombie & Fitch Co., Madison Ave. at 45th St., New York,
 N.Y. 10017

Alaska Sleeping Bag Co., 334 N.W. 11th Ave., Portland, Oreg.
 97209

Eddie Bauer, 417 E. Pine at Summit, Seattle, Wash. 98122

L. L. Bean, Inc.; 286 Main St.; Freeport, Maine 04032

Camp and Trail Outfitters, 112 Chambers St., New York, N.Y.
 10007

Camper Kitchen Company, Box 6062, San Antonio, Tex. 78209
 (The ready-made kitchen box)

Colorado Outdoor Sports Corporation, P.O. Box 5544, Denver,
 Colo. 80217

Don Gleason's, 9 Pearl Street, Northampton, Maine 01060

Gerry, Inc.; Box 910; Boulder, Colo. 80301

Herter's, Inc.; Waseca, Minn. 56685

Himalayan Industries, P.O. Box 950, Monterey, Calif. 93942

Lightweight Camping Equipment. 112 Chambers St., New York, N.Y. 10007

Laacke & Joys Company, 1433 N. Water Street, Milwaukee, Wis. 53202

Recreational Equipment, Inc. 1525 11th Ave., Seattle, Wash. 98122

Silva, Inc.; 702 Ridgeway St., La Porte, Ind. 46350 (Compasses)

Smilie Company, 575 Howard Street, San Francisco, Calif. 94105

The Ski Hut, 1615 University Ave., Berkeley, Calif. 94703